Waging War From Canada

Why Canada is the perfect base for
organizing, supporting, and conducting
international insurgency

by Mike Pearson
wagingwar@hotmail.com

Loompanics Unlimited
Port Townsend, Washington

Neither the author nor the publisher assumes any responsibility for the use or misuse of information contained in this book. It is sold for entertainment purposes only. Be warned!

Waging War From Canada: Why Canada is the perfect base for organizing, supporting, and conducting international insurgency
© 2001 by Mike Pearson

Published by:
Loompanics Unlimited
PO Box 1197
Port Townsend, WA 98368
Loompanics Unlimited is a division of Loompanics Enterprises, Inc.
Phone: 360-385-2230
E-mail: service@loompanics.com
Web site: www.loompanics.com

Cover by Harlan Kramer

ISBN 1-55950-219-3
Library of Congress Card Catalog Number 200193857

Contents

1

Introduction

"Canada is a Club Med for terrorists." — Texas Congressman Lamar Smith

"Our geographic location also makes Canada a favourite conduit for terrorists wishing to enter the United States, which remains the principal target for terrorist attacks worldwide." — Canadian Senate Committee

"By way of example, the following terrorist groups or front groups acting on their behalf have been and are active in Canada: Hezbollah and other Shiite Islamic terrorist organizations; several Sunni Islamic extremist groups, including Hamas, with ties to Egypt, Libya, Algeria, Lebanon and Iran; the Provisional IRA; the Tamil Tigers; the Kurdistan Worker's Party (PKK); and all of the world's major Sikh terrorist groups." — Ward Elcock, Director of the Canadian Security Intelligence Service

Waging War From Canada
Why Canada is the perfect base for organizing, supporting,
and conducting international insurgency

2

Scope of Terrorist Activity in Canada

Canada is a peaceful, polite country which experiences a mere fraction of the violent crime enjoyed by its American neighbour. Furthermore, Canadian nationals, military personnel, and institutions are seldom the target of terrorist attacks. Yet, according to a recent Canadian Security Intelligence Service report, "Terrorist Groups are present here whose origins lie in virtually every significant regional, ethnic, and nationalist conflict there is: the Punjab; the Israeli-Palestinian conflict; Egyptian, Algerian, and Sudanese unrest; Lebanon; Turkey; Northern Ireland; Sri Lanka; the former Yugoslavia and Afghanistan." For a number of reasons, religious, political, and nationalist groups have used Canada as their operational headquarters or as an important base of operations.

A few recent examples of organizations waging war from Canadian soil are:

- *Al-Qaeda:* In December of 1999, Ahmed Ressam was caught smuggling a hundred pounds of liquid RDX and four detonation devices from Canada to the United States, where he was headed to help ring in the New Year with a bang. He was later identified as an agent of Al-Qaeda, the anti-American group financed by Osama bin Laden. Ressam had come to Canada as a refugee claimant. His claim was denied, but Canadian immigration authorities did not act on his deportation warrant. Neither did Montreal police when he was subsequently arrested for auto theft.

- *Babbar Khalsa:* In one of the most successful military operations ever conducted on Canadian soil, Sikh operatives planted a bomb on an Air India flight leaving from a Canadian airport. Three hundred and twenty-nine people were killed. Canadian Police and Intelligence investigations into the matter have been worthy of the Keystone Kops. Charges have been repeatedly laid, but so far there have been no convictions.

- *Hezbollah:* American Intelligence revealed that Hani Al-Sayegh was a chief suspect in the Al Khobar bombing which killed 19 U.S. soldiers. During the time he was exposed by American Intelligence, Mr. Al-Sayegh was studying English literature at a Canadian University.

- *Al Jihad:* One of the major leaders of the Vanguards of Conquest, the armed military wing of Al Jihad, was revealed to be Mohamed Zeki Mahjoub. He was conducting his leadership from Toronto, Canada, having entered the country years ago on a forged Saudi passport.

- *Liberation Tigers of Tamil Eelam:* The translator hired to assist a Royal Canadian Mounted Police investigation into Tamil Tiger activity in Canada was later revealed to be a high-ranking Tiger commander. The Mounties complained that he lied to them during his security check.

- *Mohawk Warrior Society:* In the early 1990s, Mohawk warriors turned to armed struggle, shooting down a U.S. National Guard helicopter, killing a Canadian kop who charged their fortified positions, and forced local politicians into hiding. When the Canadian army surrounded their positions, leading militants escaped amidst the confusion of a staged civilian demonstration.

Waging War From Canada
Why Canada is the perfect base for organizing, supporting,
and conducting international insurgency

4

Why Canada?

While there have been some stunning military successes organized or conducted in Canada, most organizations operating in Canada use it mainly as a base for supporting organizational and logistic purposes. Whether seeking to fundraise, launch an international propaganda campaign, or merely looking for a convenient location from which to hit the Great Satan, Canada is an excellent base of operations. It has unique advantages for those engaged in the whole range of organizational activities:

- *Fundraising.* Canada is a wealthy, industrial society with many advantages for fundraisers. There is no equivalent to the American Antiterrorism and Effective Death Penalty Act, meaning front groups may legally receive funds for their struggle. Moreover, properly constituted front groups can register as charities and raise money tax-free, with no need to launder the proceeds. A fifth of Canadians were born outside Canada, and there are expatriate and immigrant communities from all over the world from whom war-taxes or sympathetic donations may be levied. Canada has many public spending programs, which are easily defrauded by determined organizations. Its undefended 4,000 mile-long border with the United States was custom-made for smuggling illegal aliens and drugs.

- *Safe Haven.* Canada accepts a far higher proportion of immigrants from all over the world, and aims to increase its population by one percent per year by doing so. Most operatives, however, enter Canada through their generous refugee program. Under this program, anyone from anywhere in the world may claim refugee status with or without identification. Very few of them are detained, and from that moment, they may rightfully receive free legal advice, healthcare, and economic assistance. Once operatives are in Canada, they may easily create a false Canadian identity with which to enter the United States or simply cross the border by stealth. Deportation orders for those who enter or remain in Canada illegally are seldom acted upon. For those with serious legal troubles back home, Canada provides a safe haven: it has no death penalty and usually will not extradite people facing it in another jurisdiction.

- *Operational support.* There is no Canadian equivalent to the American Central Intelligence Agency or British Secret Service. Policing and Intelligence are conducted by dozens of various agencies, ministries, civilian and military bodies. Communication among them is poor, to the extent that they often refuse to cooperate or share information about operatives and organizations working in Canada. Moreover, all of the important ones are under direct political control. This makes Canada a relatively safe place from which to support overseas branches of an organization. It is for this reason that various Sikh groups have moved their operational headquarters from India to Canada, and why some American libertarian groups maintain their arms dumps on Canadian rather than American soil.

- *Military support and supply.* As America's largest trading partner and trusted ally, Canadian institutions have access to virtually all technologies, industrial processes, and "dual-use" chemical and biological agents. Moreover, these products and the knowledge required to utilize them are far less strictly controlled in Canada than they are in the U.S. For this reason, dozens of organizations have created clandestine procurement and shipping networks to

Waging War From Canada
Why Canada is the perfect base for organizing, supporting,
and conducting international insurgency

6

obtain knowledge and material not easily available in America or impossible to obtain in their home countries.

- *Military operations.* Canada's proximity to the United States makes it an excellent base from which to conduct military operations against targets in that country. In such cases, official investigation is made more difficult if the suspects are in a different national jurisdiction. It was for this reason — and the ease of creating false Canadian identification — that the World Trade Center bombers intended to escape back to Canada after conducting their operation. Canada hosts many international academic, business, and diplomatic conventions where targets of opportunity regularly present themselves — and they are almost always more lightly guarded than they would be at home. Should military operations go wrong, those who are arrested face far less chance of conviction in Canada than in most countries, and far more lenient sentences if they should be convicted.

- *Information warfare and Propaganda.* Canada's communication infrastructure is irretrievably wedded to American infrastructure, yet the laws and safeguards surrounding its misuse are far less stringent. It is also an internationally engaged "middle-power" with unique susceptibilities to well-designed propaganda. If skillfully conducted, Canadian propaganda campaigns can produce alliances and solidarity which would make almost all operations untouchable in Canada and much more credible with international agencies and foreign governments.

Purpose of This Book

The purpose of this book is threefold:

1. To provide background information on why Canada is an excellent place from which to organize and conduct fundraising, recruiting, propaganda, information-warfare, and military campaigns.

2. To explain how insurgents use the particularities and weaknesses of Canada to further a cause, using examples from successful organizations currently active in Canada.

3. To point readers toward further resources and reliable sources of information.

In fulfilling these objectives, the author makes no judgments of any organization. The words "terrorist," "freedom fighter," "insurgent," "soldier," "warrior," and "operative" are used interchangeably and without bias. If their cause is just, Godspeed. If it is not, may they burn in Hell. Either way, Canada is an excellent place from which to advance said cause.

Chapter One
Overview: Canadian Geo-Politics

"To condemn these people, to call them terrorists, is anti-Canadian. There is Irish blood coursing through my veins, but that doesn't mean I am a member of the IRA." — Canada's Liberal Minister of Finance Paul Martin defending his participation at a FACT fundraiser

Geography

With the exception of Russia, Canada is the largest country in the world. Stretching from the Atlantic Ocean in the East to the Pacific Ocean in the West, from the Arctic Ocean in the North to the Great Lakes in the South, it is just really, really big. Canada has swamps bigger than Texas and electoral districts the size of France.

Canadians are proud of the size of their country, but the fact is, the majority of it is composed of rock, scrub, tundra, and permafrost that isn't fit for a dog to live in. Except for a few scattered villages, the North is virtually unpopulated, and the

Waging War From Canada
Why Canada is the perfect base for organizing, supporting,
and conducting international insurgency

10

vast majority of Canadians live huddled along the Great
Lakes, along the Northeastern American border. It is there that
the population is concentrated, and it is there that you will find
the largest cities. It is there that the vast majority of immigrants and refugees from Asia, Africa, Eastern Europe, and
the Middle East settle. It is there that it is easiest to go underground, raise funds, organize, launch information warfare, or
prepare for a military campaign.

Some operatives have tried to use Canada's rural communities and vast wastelands for cover. This is generally a bad idea.
In the sparsely populated areas of Canada — almost all of
Canada — newcomers stand out like dreadlocks at a Klan
rally. Here are a few examples to prove my point:

- *Sikh and ye shall find.* The Sikh freedom fighters who
  pulled off the 1985 Air India bombing first tested their
  technology outside a backwater town in the Rocky Mountains. Their test detonations were observed by the Canadian Security Intelligence Service. They have only the incompetence of the Royal Canadian Mounted Police, their
  own smarts, and the particularities of the Canadian justice
  system to thank for the fact that, so far, there have been no
  convictions. By contrast, anti-abortionist bombers in Toronto tested their technology in a downtown park. Nobody
  saw a thing, and the kops chalked it up to a childish prank
  before heading back to the donut shop.

- *Waco North.* Weibo Ludwig, who is currently in prison,
  set up a compound in outback Alberta. He thought he
  would be far from the prying eyes of the Antichrist and
  The Man. Old Weibo didn't like oil companies, but it
  turned out that the brother-in-arms who helped him bomb
  them was a Mountie. The RCMP were on him like a dirty

shirt; he stood out too much among the local yokels. In downtown Toronto or Montreal he would have just been another Jesus-freak among millions of people, and not worth surveilling.

- *Hillbilly Jihad.* On the eve of the millennium, Ahmed Ressam got caught crossing into America with a hundred pounds of liquid RDX and four detonators. American INS men admitted the only reason they caught him was that he was crossing at a country border post. If he'd crossed from near his base of Montreal — Canada's second largest city — he would almost certainly have made it, as he and his cronies had several times before. He's not doing much for his cause from a Yankee prison, and you can bet Allah is pretty pissed off that his boy didn't read this Geography Lesson.

A Geography Lesson

Insurgents should work from the cities. In general, this means along the 401 Highway from Windsor to Quebec City along the Northeastern border of the United States. In particular, this means the cities of Montreal and Toronto (Vancouver, on the Pacific Ocean and on the other side of the country, is a notable exception). About half of the people in the cities along the 401 are newcomers from all over the world, whereas the rest of the country tends to be fifth generation white. Nobody stands out in Toronto or Montreal.

If the goal is to organize volunteers or simply raise a war-tax from among the expatriates, operatives are far more likely to find sympathetic candidates in the major cities.

Waging War From Canada
Why Canada is the perfect base for organizing, supporting,
and conducting international insurgency

12

If the goal is to carry out information warfare, it is there that the warrior will find the infrastructure.

If the goal is to take out a target of opportunity, it is along the 401 that terrorists will find the international airports, universities, convention centres, and diplomatic missions where they will be arriving.

If the goal is to legally or illegally raise funds, it is in the cities along the Great Lakes and St. Lawrence River that most of the country's wealth can be found.

If the goal is to make agitation-propaganda, it is here that the operative will find the centres of opinion.

If the goal is to attack Uncle Sam, the warrior will find a very busy border crossing a few miles away.

If the goal is to obtain dual-use chemical or biological agents, or the knowledge of how to use them, it is near Toronto and Montreal that terrorists will find centres of research and high-tech industry.

If the goal is to go underground, there is no place like a large urban centre. The infinite wasteland of small towns and bush, which compose the Canadian hinterland can't hide a warrior quite as well as the alleys, mosques, sprawling sub-urbs, and ethnic neighbourhoods of Toronto. Even if a lone-wolf just plans to mail letter bombs to his favourite CEO, he'll have an easier time from along the 401. In the outback, the postmaster will remember "that quiet fella who mails a lot of parcels." Canada is a land of wilderness, but there is no reason to go there unless the terrorist wants to try out his new .50 calibre sniper rifle on a moose. Even then, it would be safer in downtown Montreal trying it out on a raccoon. Better yet, try it out on an SQ (see Glossary at the end of the book).

Political Structure

Unlike its neighbour to the south, Canada never had the balls to pull off a revolution. As a result, it remains to this day a "constitutional monarchy." In other words, Canada's head of state is HRM Queen Elizabeth II, the Queen of England. Most Canadians are not of British heritage, and they realize how absurd it is to have a drunken old German tart with advanced symptoms of venereal disease as its head of state. This partly explains why Canadians instinctively tolerate national liberation struggles. If an insurgent's government is as stupid as theirs, then by all means come by and fight it. If Canadians weren't so gosh-darn nice, they would do the same thing.

In theory, no act of parliament can become law in Canada unless the Queen's representative (the Governor-General) signs it. Currently, that representative is a woman who emigrated from China and used to have a bad TV show. Before that, it was a hockey player who took too many hits in the corners. In reality, nobody gives a shit what the Governor General or the Queen thinks, and laws are made by Acts of Parliament.

Federal Parliament

Canadian parliament is bicameral (having two branches or houses), but the second house — the Senate — is unelected and composed of old party hacks that had to be bought off for services rendered. Most don't bother to attend and at least one of them draws his pay cheque from his home in Mexico. The primary house, the House of Commons, is the elected members of government and opposition parties. As will

Waging War From Canada
Why Canada is the perfect base for organizing, supporting,
and conducting international insurgency

14

become clear, it is very important for groups hoping to openly
organize and fundraise in Canada to make nice with these
parties. Or at least with the ones who have a shot at forming a
government. The main political parties are as follows:

- *Liberals:* This is the party which has held the government
  for most of the twentieth century, largely because they
  work hard to attract and keep the immigrant and non-white
  vote. Smart organizations use this in their favour and do all
  they can to see that their ex-pats work for and contribute to
  the Liberals. It is largely thanks to the Liberals' political
  control of police and intelligence agencies that Canada is
  such a good environment for operatives to work in.

  [handwritten margin note: Liberals? Thank you]

- *Canadian Reform Alliance Party (CRAP):* Western-based,
  right-wing party with Republican tendencies and a strong
  racist and law-and-order streak. Currently as the official
  opposition, they have the second highest number of
  members in government. If this party ever forms a government, it will become much harder to operate out of
  Canada. Fortunately, that will never happen because they
  can't take electoral districts which are French nor those
  that have high numbers of immigrant and non-white
  Canadians. Unless a terrorist is a pro-life white-
  supremacist Jesus-freak, these people aren't going to like
  his organization.

- *Bloc Quebecois:* Quebec-based party which seeks to de-
  clare independence from Canada. Useful ally because they
  are the only influential party which is openly subversive.
  On the other hand, operatives shouldn't get too cozy with
  them because they are all under RCMP surveillance. No
  presence outside of French-speaking Quebec.

- *Conservative Party:* Fringe party much like the Liberals but more openly corrupt. Used to be powerful until the media broke stories concerning Swiss bank accounts.

- *New Democratic Party:* Nominally socialist party, much like British Labour. No chance of ever forming a government, but they will bend over backwards to prove that they are not racist. This can be useful if the kops or spooks are cracking down on an insurgent's group. Considered the "conscience of parliament," they are more influential than their numbers would suggest. For operatives working openly in Canada (i.e., fundraising, propaganda), it's worth kicking in a few hundred dollars to their local pinko candidate.

- *Fringe Parties:* Other nationally recognized political parties include the Communists, the Marxist-Leninist Party, the Marijuana Party, and assorted other nutbars. These parties have no chance of ever gaining political influence, but in some circumstances they may be a useful source of Canadian sympathizers or connections. If a group is doing some extra-legal fundraising by shipping some BC bud to the United States, for example, the Marijuana Party can probably set them up with some growers. If the cause is class-based, the operative might find some useful idiots hanging around the Reds. But the warrior should be aware though, that all of these fringe parties are under at least nominal surveillance, usually in the form of planted informers.

Parliament, then, is composed of members elected from these parties. Whichever party has the most members elected gets to form the government. Some members of the governing party are selected to become Ministers of Cabinet, meaning

Waging War From Canada
Why Canada is the perfect base for organizing, supporting,
and conducting international insurgency

16

they oversee civil-service departments. Democracy stops here, however, because the actual members of parliament —: even from the governing party — have no power. The real power is concentrated in the Prime Minister's Office and the Privy Council. Although this little civics lesson is as boring as watching blood dry, it is vitally important to any organization larger than an underground cell working in Canada. This cannot be stressed enough: [the PMO and the Privy Council control almost all policing, criminal and security intelligence gathering, threat assessment, and foreign relations] They also control the flow of information between domestic and foreign police and intelligence agencies. Despite its democratic appearance, Canada is really a rotating dictatorship with these two small bodies at the top. If these two top bodies are passively with an insurgent, then no one can touch his organization on Canadian soil. If they are actively against an insurgent, then his organization is either screwed or condemned to operating strictly underground.

The Prime Minister's Office (PMO)

The Prime Minister is the leader of the party who has the most members elected to parliament. Currently that is Jean Chretien of the Liberals, an old-school godfather of the rough and tumble street-fights of French-Canadian politics. To give an example of his style, at a children's celebration in the capital, he charged through his own security perimeter to personally kick the shit out of a protestor. He has little command of English, a heavy speech impediment, and a remarkable resemblance to Frankenstein, but under the Canadian system of governance he rules. If operating in Canada, terrorists must not piss off the Prime Minister, his party, or his friends. The resources of the state are at their command, and if operatives don't play by the rules they will be turned against them. Worse yet, the resources of other states — notably the U.S. and Israel — will be invited to come in and do the same. If, on the other hand, the Prime Minister thinks the insurgent can influence people of his ethnicity or cause others to vote for his party, the operative is far safer than he would be in a country such as America where policing and intelligence are more independent of political control.

The Prime Minister's Office — composed of the Prime Minister, his senior staff, and Liberal party hacks — is the body that controls. Insurgents must respect them if intending to publicly organize, fundraise, or agitate.

The Privy Council

While effectively under the thumb of the PMO, the Privy Council is the elite of Canadian governance. It is composed of senior cabinet ministers, the Prime Minister, and top bureaucrats. It is ultimately responsible for most policing and intelligence. It includes the Security and Intelligence Secretariat, which has a mandate from the Prime Minister to coordinate intelligence gathering among various bodies, and the Intelligence Assessment Secretariat, which identifies and ranks security threats for the Prime Minister.

Provincial Parliaments

Canada is divided into ten geo-political divisions, each of which has a parliament much like the one described above. While these governments do have a limited role in policing

Waging War From Canada
Why Canada is the perfect base for organizing, supporting,
and conducting international insurgency

18

and the gathering of criminal intelligence, they are not nearly
as important to the discussion as the over-arching Federal
government. One exception is Quebec, Canada's French-
speaking province. Because of its active hostility to the *maudit
anglais* (God-damned English) who oppress them, the
Quebecois government attempts to engage in its own foreign
policy and threat assessment. This conflict is one of the main
reasons that Canada as a whole has never been able to agree
on a national counter-terrorism plan. This is, as we shall see, a
good thing.

Inter-agency Communication

The political culture and organization of Canada contains
many broad weaknesses, which may be exploited by freedom
fighters. Chief among these is the inability of agencies to effectively communicate criminal and intelligence data. There
are many reasons for this, all of which should be taken into
account when conducting or organizing operations in Canada:

- *Lack of coordination.* Canada has no non-partisan agency,
  such as the American Central Intelligence Agency or the
  British Secret Intelligence Service, responsible for the coordination and dissemination of security and foreign intelligence. Rather, these responsibilities are spread throughout dozens of agencies and Ministries. For example, the
  Solicitor General is responsible for assessing domestic terrorist threats, while the Minister of Foreign Affairs is responsible for assessing terror-affecting Canadians overseas. According to the anti-terrorist think-tank The
  Mackenzie Institute, this "...means instead of raw information being sent directly to an interested agency, it must

first pass through the Privy Council Office in Ottawa." If, for example, immigration officials want to talk with the RCMP "it has to go up the ladder and back down, not straight across." Well-organized groups exploit this weakness by ensuring they have influence at the top of that ladder, mainly by publicly and/or covertly supporting the Liberal Party of Canada.

- *Institutional secrecy.* Most agencies that gather intelligence on terror-related groups and individuals, including the Canadian Security Intelligence Service, Customs and Immigration, and the Department of External Affairs, are civilian agencies. The Canadian Civil Service inherited British traditions of institutional secrecy, whereby various agencies protect their databases and are reluctant to share their information with other bodies. Moreover, police and military intelligence are extremely reluctant to share information with civilian bodies. A good example of this is CPIC, the database used by police in Canada to identify criminals. The Royal Canadian Mounted Police are responsible for this database, but until recently they would not grant access to CSIS, the civilian security intelligence body. Similarly, the RCMP would not allow Canadian Immigration officers access to the database until 1998, even though they had granted American Immigration and Naturalization Service officers access years before. This secrecy extends to the members of parliament who make policy and pass legislation. Unlike American politicians, they are not briefed on intelligence matters and — except for the few who are in the Cabinet —have no greater access to such information than any other citizen.

- *Political culture.* In spite of an awareness of terrorist organizations operating on their soil, Canadians are sel-

Waging War From Canada
Why Canada is the perfect base for organizing, supporting,
and conducting international insurgency

20

dom targets of such groups and they tend to turn a blind eye. According to John Thompson, "Canadians and, by extension, Canadian politicians, just don't take any terror problem seriously. ...It is difficult for many individual citizens to accept that malevolence exists. Consequently, when political (or quasi-political) violence occurs in Canada, it is often quickly forgotten — or readily forgiven." In 1993 Mohawk Indian organizations pulled off several car bombings and drive-bys. They shot up the city hall and the customs office and forced the mayor and his family into hiding. The federal government did not intervene in the insurgency, however, until it realized it was losing millions of tax dollars on the tariffs of cigarettes smuggled by the Mohawks to finance their struggle. The political culture is such that the state will prefer blind inertia unless forced to react. For this reason, non-violent activities such as fundraising, organization, recruiting, agitation, and non-military supply are permitted to occur more or less openly and without interference.

- *Multiculturalism.* According to the former Chief of CSIS Strategic Planning, "Canada's unique policy of multiculturalism complicates matters by encouraging extremists to confuse the retaining of their cultures with the importing of what Canadian counter-terrorist officers call 'homelands violence.'" For example, the 1985 Air India bombing, which killed 329, mostly Indo-Canadians, was generally thought to be an Indian rather than a Canadian problem. This even though the headquarters of the responsible organization is located in Canada and the bomb itself was placed on board the plane in a Canadian airport. About one out of every five Canadians were born in another country, and this constituency forms a large part of the support of the powerful Liberal party. As a result, politicians and agencies are extremely frightened of accusations of racism if they should be seen to delve into any organization whose membership is of a specific ethnicity. The Minister of Finance, the second-most powerful politician in Canada, recently called it "anti-Canadian" to investigate ethnically composed organizations, and Canada's national newspaper has been chilled by a huge lawsuit in which a front group claims the paper is "racist" for its investigations into fundraising for the LTTE. Official and private bodies are reluctant to collect, share, or be associated with any ethnicity-based information. If fighting a national liberation struggle from Canada, a skillful exploitation of official multiculturalism is one of the freedom fighter's greatest shields.

Thanks Pierre Trudeau For That
Now they use This
Liberal Policy To carry
Out and organize Terrorism

Chapter Two
Getting Into Canada

"Even when a [Canadian] refugee claim is denied and the alien ordered deported, the deportation order is almost never carried out." — Texas Congressman Lamar Smith

"Foreign-based terrorist organizations have been attracted to establishing themselves in Canada for a number of reasons. One of these is the fact that it is not only very easy to get into the refugee determination system in the first place but, unless there is very obvious adverse information available on an individual, no security check is usually made until a claim is accepted and application is made for landed immigrant status." — Martin Collacott, Canadian Department of External Affairs

"If someone skips a refugee hearing in Quebec and moves into Ontario, it may take weeks (if ever) before Immigration Officers in Ontario learn of it. For their part, those who duck their hearings usually will have ...sufficient ID for almost all purposes in North America." — John Thompson, Director, Mackenzie Institute

Waging War From Canada
Why Canada is the perfect base for organizing, supporting,
and conducting international insurgency

24

Before enjoying the many advantages that Canada has to offer their strong arms and willing hearts, terrorists need to get here. There are four basic methods of entering Canadian territory, each of which is discussed in more detail below:

- *Visitor:* This includes coming as a tourist, a student, or on a temporary work visa. If the goal in coming to Canada is just to pull off a quick hit, put some fear of the Lord into the ex-pat community, or sneak into the U.S., this might meet the insurgent's needs. There are over a hundred million border crossings by land in any given year and virtually all of them are successful. Another million short-term visa applications are made by visitors coming by air or by sea each year. About 90% of these are successful.

- *Refugee claimant:* By far the most common method for operatives to enter Canada is as a refugee claimant. Anyone landing in Canada has the right to make such a claim, regardless of their country of origin. Better yet, no identification is required and it provides instant legal access to Canadian healthcare, Canadian identification, and Canadian welfare benefits. There is the option of actually making a claim, (which may take several years before one is legally entitled to live in Canada), or of abandoning the claim. About 20,000 people per year make refugee claims in Canada. According to a United States House of Representatives committee report, about half of those claims are abandoned by people who "disappear into Canadian society each year never to be located by law enforcement authorities. Those who are caught are rarely, if ever, deported from Canada."

- *Immigration:* If he needs to work in Canada for the long term, needs to work openly, and isn't likely to make a convincing refugee claim, then the operative will want to become a permanent resident. Canada aims to increase its population 1% per year by immigration, and about 77% of all applications are successful. There are many categories of immigrants, each with their own rules and their own methods of getting around the rules.

- *Illegal migration:* Canada has thousands of miles of coastline on three oceans, and some folks just make like the Mayflower and land here. This worked like a charm until the mid-1980s, but nowadays it's not as easy as it sounds. If already in the United States, however, entering Canada illegally is a cakewalk. And vice versa. *Roxham Road*

Visiting Canada as a Tourist

Canada has many attractions of interest to travelers, sightseers, and freedom fighters. There are the Great Lakes, of course, with their sparkling waters and loosely guarded nuclear power stations. There are the charming folkways of the aboriginal territories, where a visitor may buy a traditional Mohawk dream catcher or rocket-propelled grenade. There is the stark beauty of the prairies, dotted with farmer's cooperatives selling tracer-free ammonium nitrate and diesel oil. Then, of course, there is the nightlife of the big cities. The largest of these, Toronto and Montreal, have dazzling theatre districts and are only a ten hour drive from the World Trade Center. With excellent rates on van rentals and oodles of that famous Canadian hospitality, shouldn't an insurgent plan his next vacation in what an early explorer called "the land God gave to Cain"?

Waging War From Canada
Why Canada is the perfect base for organizing, supporting,
and conducting international insurgency

26

If living in a country where a visa is required to come to Canada, here's what the terrorist needs to bring to the nearest Canadian consulate:

1. A valid passport or travel document — valid enough, at least, to fool a bored staffer who just wants to get the paperwork done so he can go for his next smoke-break.

2. Enough money to support himself during his stay. Anything less than $200.00 Canadian per day of the trip is likely to attract attention.

3. A stated intention to stay in Canada for a temporary period. It is necessary to do a little research so there is a realistic travel plan. Common tourist destinations are Vancouver (Pacific), Niagara Falls (Central), or Halifax (Atlantic).

4. Completed application form.

5. Payment of a non-refundable processing fee.

That's it. The vast majority of applications are approved. One should know, however, that a Canadian immigration officer has the discretion to refuse entry even if the insurgent has a visa, if the officer has reason to believe there isn't an intention to leave when the visa expires. If questioned, the insurgent should use the immigration officer's prejudices against him. He should act like a stupid tourist and stick to the story given on the visa application. If visiting someone, he should make it a friend rather than a relative. Definitely not a comrade.

Studying in Canada

Canadian universities love foreign students, because the tuition rates they pay are up to seven times greater than those paid by Canadians. They are the economic lifeblood of Cana-dian colleges, universities, and technical schools. They want students. Moreover, Canada is academically and technologi-cally advanced and there are legitimate reasons for attending Canadian universities beyond entry into Canada. Well-organized and funded forces are sure to have a few bright young brain-workers studying organic chemistry at McGill or Computer Science at Waterloo. That is intelligence gathering in the purest sense. A recently leaked CSIS report lists foreign students studying in Canada as the chief means by which op-eratives acquire dual-use chemical and biological agents, as well as the knowledge required to utilize those substances. According to that report, "The presence of foreign students... at our academic institutions, research organizations, interna-tional conferences, and high-technology companies will re-main an efficient means of acquiring technical expertise in fields of dual-use applicability."

In addition to the requirements mentioned above for a basic tourist visa, a foreign student is required to obtain a letter of acceptance from a Canadian college or university. He or she may also be required to submit a medical check and a police background/security check. If one is well-prepared, that need not be as daunting as it sounds. After working on the 1996 Al-Khobar bombing, which killed 19 American soldiers, for ex-ample, Hani Al-Sayegh fled to Canada as a foreign student. He studied English literature for some reason. He must have already passed his chemistry exams.

Waging War From Canada
Why Canada is the perfect base for organizing, supporting,
and conducting international insurgency

28

Temporary Work Visa

It is very complicated to obtain a temporary work visa. The requirements are in constant flux and depend upon a number of variables: international treaties, citizenship, the Canadian labor market, availability of government programs, and a dozen other factors. Still, if a terrorist has some greatly demanded skill — generally in information or high-technology — it is a way to set foot in Canada. The likeliest method of success is the terrorist is actually hired by a Canadian employer, who will then untangle the paperwork from there. There are much easier and less monitored ways to get into Canada, however, and this isn't likely to be a realistic method of entry for most fighters. For sympathetic researchers, academics, and scientists, however, this may be an excellent way to acquire dual-purpose or prohibited chemicals and technology. Depending on who or what the enemy is, this may also be an excellent way to gain intelligence from the inside.

Coming to Canada as a Refugee

According to the Canadian Senate Committee on Terrorism and Public Safety, the vast majority of "terrorists and other security threats gaining entry to Canada come as refugee claimants." Anyone arriving in Canada from anywhere in the world has a right to make a refugee claim, even if they are travelling on false identification or with no identification at all. The moment they state their claim to an immigration officer, they enjoy all the legal protections of a Canadian citizen — they may not be searched, and they are instantly entitled to free healthcare and welfare payments. Moreover, people entering via this method do not have to undergo the messy business of preliminary background checks they might need if entering on a visa or as an immigrant. Except in rare cases, refugee claimants are free to live and do whatever they please in Canada for the year or more that it takes for their claim to be heard. Should their claim be eventually denied, there is not much chance they will be deported. It is largely Canada's handling of refugee claimants that made a Texas Congressman call Canada a "Club Med" for terrorists. This is completely unfair, of course, because Club Meds don't get nearly as much snow.

Claiming Refugee Status

To claim refugee status, one just shows up at a Canadian airport or point of entry and tells the Customs and Immigration agent (one must speak slowly, for they are not very bright), "I claim refugee status." It's that simple. The only people who are not permitted to claim refugee status are those for whom a deportation order has previously been made.

The Customs agent will whisk the claimant away into a barren little room and try to interrogate him. There is no need to answer any of his questions, nor should he. Anything said will be used against him at the refugee hearing which will follow. There is no need to show identification or to even have identification. Seventy-five percent of people making refugee claims in Canada have "improper" identification — half of those have no identification at all. This is usually because they destroyed it en route — usually by ripping it to pieces and flushing it down the airline toilet. If wanted in the mother country or anywhere else in the world, this is a very good idea.

The Customs agent does have the right to take one's fingerprints, and they will. However, a senate committee on the sub-

Partam Roo

Waging War From Canada
Why Canada is the perfect base for organizing, supporting,
and conducting international insurgency

30

ject found that "the quality of prints is poor because of inadequate training and equipment — and, in any event, fingerprints are warehoused unless a problem with a particular claimant arises." The Al Qaeda fighter Ahmed Ressam was fingerprinted as a refugee claimant, but those prints were never correlated to those taken upon his criminal arrest for auto-theft nor his successful Canadian passport application.

At this point, the vast majority of refugee claimants are released, and entitled to work in Canada and take advantage of the many social programs. Theoretically, the claimant will be detained if wanted in another country for a serious criminal offence, but if that is the case, he will have probably, as is his right, not have given a real name. Unless his mugshot is on the FBI or Interpol "most-wanted" list, the claimant will almost certainly be free to go. In most cases, the only conditions on that release are that the claimant provide a Canadian address once one has been established and that he show up for his hearing before the Immigration and Refugee Board of Canada. The refugee claimant should agree to those conditions whether or not he intends to honour them. As the department itself admits, "there is no effective system in place to verify compliance with these terms and conditions. Thousands of persons awaiting inquiry or removal are physically in Canada, and thousands of others have voluntarily left the country, but the department is not aware of their whereabouts."

Welcome to Canada!

The Immigration and Refugee Board of Canada

Canada is a signatory to the United Nations Convention Relating to the Status of Refugees. This convention defines a refugee as anyone who faces serious persecution on the basis of their race, religion, nationality, membership in a social group, or political opinion. Under the convention, Canada is obliged to offer sanctuary to anyone who meets this definition. Many other countries have signed this agreement, but none interpret or administer it as liberally as Canada. The body responsible for deciding on refugee claims is an embarrassing collection of troughers known as the Immigration and Refugee Board of Canada.

Probably the best job in Canada is to sit on the Immigration and Refugee Board of Canada (IRB). It is a purely political patronage appointment, meaning that no qualifications are required. You get the job because the cabinet says you should, and that is that. Once appointed, you get about $90,000 a year to hear a few cases a week. You get fawned over like a judge, a nice office to play Windows Freecell in, and all the perks and prestige that go along with the position. Since it is a purely political appointment, the type of people appointed to the board (and there are hundreds of such appointments) change with the government of the day. Still, the board is generally composed of the following:

1. Political party hacks, fundraisers, enforcers, and envelope lickers who have to be rewarded for their election work but can't be trusted to an appointment that requires any level of competency.

2. Do-gooders, refugee advocates, and ethnic power brokers. It pisses off the police to no end that many people appointed to the board are actively biased in favour of all refugees or in favour of refugee claimants coming from their ancestral homelands. For governments, though, it is a good way to silence damaging criticism from "multicultural" groups. Nothing like a wheelbarrow full of money and a corner office to silence the most active critics.

Waging War From Canada
Why Canada is the perfect base for organizing, supporting,
and conducting international insurgency

32

3. Various rounders, potential blackmailers, boy-toys, mistresses, nieces and nephews of the governing members. People who cabinet ministers want to have a comfortable living but are too stupid to get a real job.

Depending on the terrorist's country of origin, he may be lucky enough to avoid the Refugee Board hearing altogether by participating in an "expedited" process. If he is offered this option — as thousands of Somalians were in the early 1990s — he should take it. It will mean that he has to tell his sad, sad story to civil servants rather than political appointees, and if he is the least bit convincing, their decision to accept his claim will be rubber-stamped. He is now a refugee with the same legal status as a landed immigrant, and well on his way to being a Canadian citizen if that is his wish.

If he is not offered an expedited process, a refugee hearing claim will be scheduled. Because of a growing backlog of about 30,000 cases, his hearing will not likely be held for a year or more after the time he first came to Canada. No matter what he does during that year he cannot be deported without his claim being heard, so he need not be afraid to work for the cause.

When the day comes for the refugee hearing, and if the claimant actually shows up (thousands do not), the claimant will be provided with a lawyer paid by the government. The Board will be represented by a lawyer who is an employee of the government, and the case will generally be decided by three of the appointees described above. It is important to note that this is a hearing and not a trial. It is "non-adversarial." The rules are much looser than they would be for a real trial and the proceedings are much less formal. This is probably because most of the Board appointees are too clueless, hungover, or apathetic to follow the sort of complicated rules followed by real judges.

The Board has two incentives to accept any person before them as a refugee claimant. The first of these is that negative decisions have to be justified in writing, whereas positive ones do not. Thus, it is simply less work to accept a refugee claimant. The Board members are generally very lazy people, and writing up decisions can take hours or even days of real work. Unless a case is obviously silly, some members will never vote "no" simply because they can't stand the thought of having to write "why."

The second reason is related to the first. Written decisions might be scrutinized by people who understand administrative law, which most Board members do not. Every sentence might be scrutinized for errors in argument, reasons for appeal, incorrect information or, worst of all, signs of racism. The members of the Board don't generally have as high a level of education or literacy as the lawyers and activists who advocate on behalf of refugees. They live in terror of scrutiny and criticism, because if they are criticized too many times, they might not get re-appointed at the end of their contracts. That is the worst possible thing that could happen to a Refugee Board Member, because it means they have to find a (shudder) job. This fear is used by skillful claimants. One lawyer has success in front of the Refugee Board largely based on his ability to casually drop into the hearing an implied relationship between himself and one of the Minister of Immigration's senior flunkies. Works like a charm.

Claim Denied

If an insurgent's claim does fail, he has several options, all of which have a high rate of success:

Waging War From Canada
Why Canada is the perfect base for organizing, supporting,
and conducting international insurgency

34

1. *Appeal.* The decision may be appealed on legal grounds to
   the Federal Court of Canada. There may be other legal
   grounds for appeal, however. He should discuss the matter
   with his lawyer, who is billing the government and not the
   operative.

2. *Ignore the decision and remain in Canada.* According to a
   report prepared by the United States House of Representatives, "10,000 refugee claimants disappear into Canadian
   society every year, never to be located by law enforcement
   authorities. Those who are caught are rarely, if ever, deported from Canada. More than 40,000 deportation orders
   have accumulated over the past six years with little action
   from Canadian authorities." Personally, I think their numbers are a bit high, but the point is valid.

3. *Ignore the decision and go to the United States.* Why not
   start a new life in the land of the brave and the home of the
   homeless? For many people making refugee claims in
   Canada, the whole point is to gain easy access to the
   United States, either because they want to live there or because they have targets there. It is easier to enter the U.S.
   from Canada than it is from any other country. As the
   American Department of Justice says, the U.S./Canada
   border is "porous."

4. *Appeal on humanitarian and compassionate grounds.* If it
   is important to an operative or his organization that he
   obtain the right to legally remain in Canada, he may appeal
   his case to the Minister of Immigration, who may then
   overturn the decision on compassionate grounds. This is
   admittedly a desperate last chance, but it does sometimes
   work. It is particularly effective in cases where the person
   has an organization behind him and a plausible propa-

ganda angle that will gain broader Canadian sympathy. As I write this, a Chinese woman who killed her husband in Canada has taken sanctuary in a Church in Kingston and is asking the Minister to waive her deportation on the grounds that China could execute her for her crime. Media and social justice types are lining up in support of her and her brave new husband. It is only a matter of time before her request is granted. Similarly, in 2000 an Arab who took sanctuary in Toronto's Church of Lebanon had his deportation order lifted on compassionate grounds in spite of the fact that he had defrauded Canadian welfare of $43,000.

Immigrating to Canada

Not everyone, of course, who comes to live in Canada comes as a refugee claimant. The vast majority of new Canadians legally immigrated there under one of several immigration programs. Canada was built on immigration and continues to accept a higher number of immigrants than almost every other country in the world. The government policy is to accept each year a number of immigrants equivalent to one percent of the existing population. With the possible exception of candidates who speak English or French, who are slightly favoured over those who do not, there is no racial bias to selecting Canadian immigrants as there generally is in Europe.

There are reams of regulations and requirements for all the various immigration programs, which I will not attempt to replicate here. All of it is available online. Those interested can go to a search engine such as www.yahoo.ca and type in "Government of Canada." From there, they can go to the main page of the Department of Immigration and follow the links to

Waging War From Canada
Why Canada is the perfect base for organizing, supporting,
and conducting international insurgency

36

the various publications on immigration programs. What follows is a summary of those programs.

Independent

Independent immigrants are those deemed to have the "right stuff" to be Canadians. Points are awarded to applicants on the basis of education, training, experience, occupational demand, arranged employment, age, knowledge of French or English, personal suitability, and family already in Canada. A certain number of spots are awarded each year and whoever has the most points among the applicants get them.

Business Immigrants

If a terrorist or his organization has a lot of money he is willing to invest in Canada, he may jump to the head of the line as a Business Class Immigrant. In other words, he can more or less buy the right to immigrate. This is the normal route of Triad members. There are several subcategories of business immigration, each with their own requirements. These include investors, entrepreneurs, self-employed, and family business sponsored.

Family Sponsored

If the insurgent already has immediate family members who are permanent residents or citizens in Canada, and they have enough money to post a bond, he may immigrate without meeting all the normal requirements. His spouse may also sponsor his immigration, and this route is often used by operatives. See the section below on "Marrying a Canadian."

Live-in Caregiver

There is a special program, which allows nannies and live-in caregivers, often from the Philippines, to immigrate to Canada. Under this program, applicants must effectively agree to live in indentured servitude for two years to some yuppie lawyer and his wife. Probably not suitable to those of a terrorist temperament.

Marrying a Canadian

One subcategory of the Family Sponsored Immigration Program is spousal sponsorship. In other words, a person may be granted permanent residency without meeting the normal immigration requirements if he marries a Canadian or a permanent resident of Canada. This program is extremely useful for operatives who wish to set up fast and legal residency in Canada.

The best way to marry a Canadian, of course, is to seduce one, make a proposal on bended knee, and honeymoon in the new country where each will live happily ever after. If that is not possible, one may wish to take more of a mercenary approach.

There are Canadians who will marry anyone for money. The RCMP recently busted a scheme at a Canadian university where students' marriages were being arranged *en masse* by an international smuggling operation. Individual Canadians seeking this sort of arrangement often advertise the fact in the

Waging War From Canada
Why Canada is the perfect base for organizing, supporting,
and conducting international insurgency

38

classified ads of urban alternative weeklies. A dead give away
are the words "marriage-minded single."

One should expect to pay a lot to marry a Canadian —
$30,000 minimum, plus expenses. The reason is that the
marriage must be convincing. If immigration officials are
suspicious of a person's motives — and they often are — they
will go over every detail of the relationship and the wedding
with a fine-toothed comb. They do not have to grant a
person's immigration, and they will not unless they are
convinced. The perfect wedding will be complete with photo
albums, invitations, and the normal memorabilia and detritus
that would accompany a wedding in one's and/or one's
spouses' culture. Furthermore, they will take perverse joy in
interrogating one individually on intimate details of one's
wedding night, personal habits, family, and anything else they
can think of to trip one up. At the very least, one and one's
new spouse should hole up in a hotel for a couple of weeks to
get familiar with each other and to rehearse every detail of
one's story. While not absolutely mandatory, it does not hurt
for the sake of credibility to actually have sex. Don't worry —
having sex with a Canadian is not necessarily as bad as it
sounds.

Entering Canada Illegally

Some people just can't stand all this bureaucracy and official mumbo-jumbo, and they come to Canada the way God
intended: by darting across the American border or landing by
sea.

Canada has always had — and still does have — a trickle of
disgruntled seamen jumping ship in Canadian ports. All
coastal countries experience the same thing. The first modern,

large-scale and covert landing, however, occurred twenty years ago. A cargo ship full of "boat people" landed in a New-foundland outport. They asked the dazed villagers they encountered for a taxi to Toronto, not realizing they were on an island and that Toronto was thousands of miles away.

Everyone owes a huge debt of gratitude to those original boat people. After they were apprehended, they mounted a legal challenge, in which the Supreme Court of Canada decided that Section 7 of the Charter Rights and Freedoms (namely, that everyone is entitled to life, liberty, and security), applies to anyone who manages to set foot on Canadian soil. Thus, if a fighter can get here illegally and he is caught, he will have all the legal rights and protections afforded a Canadian. It's a good start.

Since then, there have been many other landings of boat people. In 1999, several ships full of Chinese landed on Canada's West Coast. They were detected and many were detained until their refugee claims could be heard. Many who were not detained managed to slip across the border to the U.S., but those who were detained were mostly deported. The government demonstrated it would play hardball with people entering by boat in an organized fashion. The Minister of Immigration even did a tour of the Chinese Fujian Province to persuade people how awful Canada was and why they shouldn't come here. This caused great amusement in both Canada and in China.

The fact is, with modern satellite technology, signals intelligence, and port traffic control, it is pretty difficult to land a cargo ship on the Canadian coast without someone noticing. Of course, those on the ship can still make refugee claims, but their chances of success are not as good as if they had arrived by airplane. Their chances of being detained, on the other hand, are much higher.

Chapter Three
Policing and Intelligence

"...the intelligence Canada receives may be filtered through the prism of other nations' domestic and foreign policies." — Canadian Senate Committee

"inept" — Canadian military report assessing the Quebec police (quoted in *Parameters*)

Canada is a good base from which to organize, fund, and launch struggles, but not because there are no police or intelligence agents. On the contrary — the place is crawling with them. In a given city, there may be three police services active at one time, along with various foreign and domestic spooks, eavesdroppers, and semi-official informers. Each of these services has its significant weaknesses, though, and there is a huge rift of mistrust and jealousy between those responsible for gathering criminal, security, military, and foreign intelligence. The smart terrorist will exploit these weaknesses. The really smart ones have been known to turn the various services against each other. The geniuses (e.g., the high ranking Tamil

Waging War From Canada
Why Canada is the perfect base for organizing, supporting,
and conducting international insurgency

42

Tiger who got a job as a translator working on a Royal Canadian Mounted Police investigation into the Tamil Tigers) use the police and intelligence services as a source of their own intelligence. Here is a summary of who does what in Canada:

- *Criminal Intelligence:* Most cities have a municipal police force of the donut-munching variety. As seen below, they are sometimes the most feared. The larger provinces also have a Provincial Police service largely responsible for rural areas. All of Canada is policed by the Royal Canadian Mounted Police (the mounties), who also serve as municipal or provincial police in some areas. In general, communication between police forces is fairly good, but communication between criminal and security intelligence services is very poor. That is a good thing. Likewise, the various police forces are confused about their own jurisdictions and responsibilities.

- *Security Intelligence:* Years ago, the mounties were responsible for gathering intelligence about internal and external threats to the security of Canada. A scandal erupted, however, after it became known that they had burned a barn to prevent a meeting of the American Black Panthers and the Canadian FLQ (Quebec Liberation Front). After that, the mounties were officially put exclusively on the criminal beat and a new organization — the Canadian Security Intelligence Service — was formed to deal with security intelligence. The mounties didn't like it then and they still don't like it; there is a huge rift of secrecy between the two services. They refuse to share databases and sources, and have been known to destroy information rather than let it fall into the other service's hands. Both the mounties and CSIS have accused each other of being incompetent and susceptible to political pressure. Fortunately, they are both right. Better yet, CSIS agents do not have police powers and must get the Mounties to act on their intelligence. On the downside, CSIS shares openly with and relies heavily on American, Israeli, British, and other Commonwealth intelligence agencies.

- *Military Intelligence:* Gathering and assessing intelligence about military threats to Canada is the domain of the Department of National Defence and the Communications Security Establishment (CSE). These operations are the most secretive and the most competent in Canada. They are also the best supported, largely because a military threat to Canada is by definition also a military threat to the United States. The CSE also gathers non-military signals intelligence, and has a sophisticated array of electronic signals gathering systems. Much of this data is fed to American services (notably Project Echelon) for analysis.

- *Foreign Intelligence:* Information about the activities and intentions of foreign states, individuals, and organizations is gathered by a number of civilian agencies, including the Department of Foreign Affairs, Privy Council Office, and some of the services mentioned above. There is no agency equivalent to the American CIA to coordinate this intelligence, and there is little direct communication among the various bodies. The anti-terrorist Mackenzie Institute complains that "Canadians picked up from the British the habit of almost institutionalized secrecy in the civil service." Each service hordes its own secrets; the advantages of such a system to the working terrorist are obvious. Many times it has come to light that one of the services

Waging War From Canada
Why Canada is the perfect base for organizing, supporting,
and conducting international insurgency

44

knew an immigrant was an active terrorist operative but
had neglected to inform Immigration or the police. In general, the failure of such information to reach the appropriate service was a result of the politically laden and inse-
cure path (to the Privy Council and back down again to the
appropriate branch) that information must travel.

Municipal Police

Canadian cities generally have a municipal police force
whose job it is to "serve and protect" within city limits. Their
primary concern is with work-a-day criminal and highway
traffic-act violations. They bust speeders and shoplifters, investigate the odd murder, and try to get back to the donut shop
in time for the fresh-baked honey-glazed. Less educated, less
well-funded, and more visible than other police services, they
rarely represent a threat to a terrorist organization as a whole.
Conversely, they are sometimes the greatest threat to individuals in an organization. The following is a tally of strengths and
weaknesses of municipal police — so far as freedom fighters
are concerned.

Political Independence

As we shall see, more senior police and intelligence services
are under the direct control of politicians, and their operations
and information are often curtailed by this fact. With municipal forces, the opposite is true. While city kops answer to politically appointed police service boards, the municipal police
unions generally have control over these appointments. They
also have direct influence over municipal elections and take an

active role in ensuring their candidates win. The result is that the tail wags the dog; the police control their civilian masters. In the larger cities, it is generally understood that the real chief of city police is not the person hired by city council, but the person elected head of the police brotherhood.

The implications of this are far-reaching. Without fear of retribution from political masters, city police do not hesitate to open politically controversial cans of worms. A task force was initiated by Toronto Police, for example, to infiltrate Canadian gangs supporting the Tamil liberation movement. The city kops didn't care about the charges of racism which this invoked among those who sympathize with the Tigers. Had senior services initiated such a task force, it would almost certainly have folded under political pressure. As it turned out, the Toronto force remained in operation until a high-ranking Tamil Tiger came to Toronto, fixed the situation, and assured the Toronto kops there would be no more Tamil gunfights in the suburbs of Toronto. Everyone lived happily ever after.

This appalling lack of political accountability also allows municipal kops to undertake "extra-legal" activities of their own, which senior services are far less likely to do. This is especially true in the cities of Toronto and Montreal, where racist kops (hopped up on icing sugar, no doubt) have murdered several non-whites and anti-racist activists for "resisting arrest." They have also taken a predatory interest in organizations whose politics don't match their own fascist leanings, and they tend to settle such scores on the streets rather than in the courts. Propaganda, pressure, the law, and party donations have lesser effect on the behaviour of city kops than their senior counterparts, and in some circumstances this can make them a more dangerous and persistent enemy.

Waging War From Canada
Why Canada is the perfect base for organizing, supporting,
and conducting international insurgency

46

Parochialism

It is not the job of city police to worry about the Chechen liberation struggle. It is unlikely many of them could find Grozny on a map. For that matter, it is unlikely that many of them could find a map. On the whole, they are lazy and dull and don't know or care what goes on outside city limits. With some exceptions, their intelligence is limited to criminal intelligence regarding activities which take place within their jurisdiction. They do not, to be more concise, look at the big picture. This cannot be said of senior police services and intelligence agents.

The above weakness can be exploited by maintaining a separation between those individuals and branches of an organization engaged in "criminal" activities and those engaged in other endeavors. Local police will do their job of investigating crimes on their turf, but as long as those who committed them are isolated from the military, propaganda, finance, and other branches, it is unlikely that local police will make the connection or refer the matter to a senior service. While every case is unique, this generally means that if one of a group's members is busted for a crime, he should be defended as a common criminal, and not as a part of the cause or the organization. This also implies that any criminal acts a group's operatives are involved in can survive the test of search warrants on the premises of those responsible and on phone line taps without being linked to the broader struggle. Local police are permitted to use both of these investigative methods on the flimsiest of pretenses.

Access to Information

Local police do not have access to the same sources of information as their senior counterparts, and they are far less likely to effectively use all the information they do have access to. This is particularly true of immigration warrants, which locals tend not to verify out of sheer laziness. This has resulted in legions of operatives, including prominent armed Islamic Group fighters, being arrested and subsequently released by Canadian municipal kops.

The primary database used by local police — and to which they all have access from office or car — is called CPIC. This database includes licence numbers, social insurance numbers, date of birth, previous convictions, and outstanding bench warrants of anyone who has been entered into it. The database is more or less accurate, but is often two weeks to six months out of date. It is not hard to gain access to one's record or the records of those one loves; tens of thousands of civilians who work for police services or relevant ministries have access to the same database. Many of these civilians are low-paid clerks in militant unions. Think of the possibilities. It should be noted that access to CPIC records is only logged by the system if the file is e-mailed or printed. Screen dumps, queries, and copying data by hand do not trigger a record of the user who requested the record.

Arms

Municipal police are equipped with pistols, shotguns, and crowd-control equipment — including gas, rubber bullets, stun grenades, pepper spray, tasers, horses, and — of course —

Waging War From Canada
Why Canada is the perfect base for organizing, supporting,
and conducting international insurgency

48

batons. Larger cities may have tactical squads equipped with sniper and assault rifles, although such work is usually handed off to specially trained units from senior services. Experiments with giving local police more effective arms have often gone badly. In Toronto, for example, one unit was issued automatic rifles. The first chance they got to use them — a gas station robbery — two police promptly shot each other. They also shot the robber, but it was likely he just accidentally wandered into the crossfire.

As we will see in the section of this book on military operations, there is a particular fear and disdain of handguns in Canada. This extends even to police, and in some cities rookies are issued fake handguns until they have served a prescribed amount of time. These guns may be identified by a red stripe running down the back of the grip. God forbid a terrorist should ever get into a fire-fight with the kops, but if he ever does and one of them has the red stripe on his gun, he should aim for that kop's partner.

Provincial Police

The larger provinces of Canada have provincial police forces with jurisdiction inside those provinces. Besides serving as municipal police in villages and towns, which lack a local force, they are responsible for rural areas and specialized duties such as tactical response units and Indian peacekeepers. In the less populated provinces, the federal Royal Canadian Mounted Police fulfill the role of provincial police.

The provincial services an operative is most likely to encounter are the Ontario Provincial Police and the *Surete de Quebec*. Together, they have jurisdiction over the provinces of

Ontario and Quebec, provinces which contain the largest Canadian cities and the vast majority of its citizens.

The Ontario Provincial Police (OPP)

Along highways and in smaller towns, the OPP is essentially a slightly better educated, disciplined, funded, and organized version of the municipal police, and much of what has been said above applies. There are, however, some unique qualities of the OPP, which should be noted and exploited by any operatives who may come into contact with them. This is particularly true if the struggle is related to the sovereignty, politics, or claims of indigenous people.

The vast majority of OPP spend their days writing speeding tickets on stretches of highway or eating donuts and breaking up bar fights and domestic disputes in sad, grey, little Canadian towns. It is a miserable existence. The OPP does, however, have an elite level of service which operatives in Ontario should be aware of. They are likely better trained, equipped, and motivated than any police service in Canada. These are the TRU (tactical response) teams and public-order units.

The public-order units are riot police — worth mentioning because they operate at a much higher level of discipline than any of their municipal or federal counterparts. TRU teams are the equivalent of American SWAT teams, equipped with assault rifles, sniper squads, and — upon request — heavy equipment and military hardware. The usual work of TRU teams is to respond to bank robberies, hostage-takings, and the like, but they sometimes respond to politically motivated actions. One should respect them.

One of the characteristics of special OPP teams is that they generally use more force than is required. This is especially

Waging War From Canada
Why Canada is the perfect base for organizing, supporting,
and conducting international insurgency

50

true when they are opposing Indians (i.e., native Americans —
not people from Calcutta), with whom they have a particularly
antagonistic relationship. Five years ago, an OPP TRU squad
encircled an Indian community in Ipperwash, Ontario, beat
any women and children who tried to flee, and executed the
leading activist in spite of the fact that he was unarmed and
had surrendered. In the Mohawk territory of Tyendinaga, a
TRU team executed a warrant to search an activist's house by
bulldozing it and then looking through the rubble. Fortunately,
even the TRU teams seldom use such force against non-Indian
insurgents.

The willingness to use excessive, paramilitary force is the
greatest strength of the OPP. The fact that they consistently
use that force against Indians is their greatest weakness. By a
particularly Canadian irony, the OPP are responsible for the
Indian peacekeepers which police many Indian territories.
While nominally independent, peacekeepers — who are all
Indian — are really members of the OPP. As such, they have
formal and informal access to a great deal of OPP operational
plans, personnel data, and intelligence, while often sharing
private hostility to the service. The peacekeepers are the soft
underbelly of the OPP. This is a good thing for an operative to
bear in mind if his organization is attacked by Ontario's finest.

The Surete de Quebec (SQ)

The SQ, which operates only in the French-speaking province of Canada, is quite unlike any other police service. They
are fiercely nationalistic, which in the Canadian context means
not that they are patriotic Canadians, but that they despise
anyone who is not white or does not speak French. They are
more willing than any other service to form "extra-legal" pos-

---

51

---

ses, and they are more corrupt than other police services. Fortunately, they are also poorly trained, disciplined, and equipped.

The danger of the SQ is not that they gather intelligence on an organization and carry that through to arrest and prosecution, for they are quite incompetent at that sort of thing. In fact, it is for this reason that Quebec is the best place in Canada from which to launch wire-fraud and other fundraising schemes. The danger is that they beat one to death by the side of the road for not being *pur laine Quebecois*. They are notoriously racist, anti-Semitic, and pro-French, and they are not discouraged in this by the Gaullist, separatist government of Quebec. As with any gang of thugs, the SQ should be avoided whenever possible.

Fortunately, they do not have the ability to carry through on an organizational scale. Unlike the OPP TRU teams, the SQ are not an effective paramilitary threat. When tested in 1990 by a Mohawk uprising near Montreal, SQ squads attacked entrenched Mohawk positions with nothing but handguns. The first kop over the parapet died of a bad case of lead poisoning, and the rest ran away to call the army. They subsequently tried to purchase nine Leopard tanks from an American arms dealer, but were stopped by public outrage. In short, the SQ are to be feared if a person doesn't speak French and they pull him over by the side of the road on a dark night. They are less likely to successfully investigate crime than any other Canadian police force, however, making Quebec the safest province in which to conduct extra-legal activities. In a fire-fight, they lack the equipment, training, and courage to hold their ground against determined opposition.

Waging War From Canada
Why Canada is the perfect base for organizing, supporting,
and conducting international insurgency

52

The Royal Canadian Mounted Police (RCMP)

The RCMP, also known as the Mounties, were founded as a
cavalry unit to fight French-Indian insurgents in Western Canada. They remain the only police force with national jurisdiction, and they remain more militarized than all other police
services combined. In recent years, their responsibility for assessing foreign threats to security has been given over to a civilian intelligence agency, but they have always resented this
and constantly push at the boundaries. Any police service
might get involved with operatives who commit criminal acts,
but the RCMP are most likely to assault a terrorist's Canadian
structure at an organizational level. This is particularly true if
the work of the organization is spread across several
provincial jurisdictions. Moreover, if the organization is
infiltrated by the Intelligence Service (CSIS), it will likely be
the RCMP who actually make arrests and take the matter to
the Crown.

The Mounties carry a special cachet with Canadians.
They're good propaganda. Those on ceremonial duty wear the
distinct scarlet tunics; generations of children at county fairs
have been awed by the "musical ride" — a mixture of cavalry
drill and dressage. Canadian folklore is filled with stories of
Mounties going to incredible lengths in the Arctic to track
down murderers and thieves; or of their intelligence, diplo-
macy, and discretion in negotiating with Indians. The unofficial motto of the service is "the Mounties always get their
man." The official motto should be "we do not." As we shall
see, while the Mounties have inherent strengths which make
them a force to be reckoned with, they are in some ways the
weakest police service in Canada. Certainly they are the most
subject to infiltration, bean counting, and political pressure.

Access to Information

The RCMP have access to databases other police services do not, and they are more technically savvy in accessing sources of information from other departments and services. In addition to the CPIC database which all police use, the Mounties use a tracking and intelligence database called PROMIS. They deny having such a tool, mainly because they have never paid for it and the vendor is suing them for software piracy. Nevertheless, it is commonly accepted by civilian researchers that the Mounties do use this tool, and a recent series of newspaper articles has revealed that the American CIA and the Israeli Mossad both have hard-coded backdoor keys and enjoy access on demand. Something to be aware of if one's enemy is the U.S. or Israel.

Academics estimate that one out of seven people in Canada has a file in PROMIS — this is a greater proportion than the East German STASI was able to accomplish in surveilling its own population. PROMIS does not officially exist, but even if it did, Canadians would not be able to access their records under freedom of information requests as it would be exempted on the grounds of "national security." Indeed, to request to see your record in PROMIS is grounds to create a record in the database. A reporter recently had a file opened in the database for the sin of asking what make of car the Prime Minister drove.

PROMIS includes records which could not be legally kept if its existence were acknowledged. This includes intelligence from Immigration, Canadian court records, bench warrants, dispatches from Interpol and other foreign police services, and unfounded allegations made by Mounties and their informants. All an operative can do is be aware of the database; unlike

Waging War From Canada
Why Canada is the perfect base for organizing, supporting,
and conducting international insurgency

54

CPIC, it is fairly secure except for the back-door foreign hacks noted above. Few civilians have access to it and every query or alteration is logged and subject to analysis.

Informants

The Mounties have always relied on informants to gather intelligence, and they are extremely adept at recruiting, paying, training, and protecting them. This allows the service — mainly composed of white working-class men — to reach far beyond its own demographic. Too many groups have assumed immunity from police infiltration on the grounds that they are ethnically isolated. Various Indian, Sikh, Asian, and Kurd organizations have made this mistake by underestimating RCMP skill and experience at handling informants.

There are no sure-fire ways to identify informants, and a perpetual witch hunt within an organization may be just as damaging as actually having an informer. There are some warning signs, though:

- *Odd sources of income:* Payments to informers are often filtered through some other government agency. Depending on the informer's status, this often includes tax rebates, social assistance, student loans, and the like. Take, for example, an Ojibway lad who was sent to infiltrate a militant Mohawk group. He was on welfare at the time, and welfare consistently miscalculated his cheque and paid him two or three times more than he was due. This was an early warning sign, although by no means a reliable one. Lots of people involved in struggles have sources of money they don't care to talk about, and informers are sometimes paid in cash (although the RCMP accountants prefer not to). Those who are motivated by loftier motives or vengeance may not be paid at all.

- *Prison or prosecution record:* The primary recruitment ground for informers is among those charged with an offense or those serving time.

- *New in town:* Informers arc usually deployed a long way from home. Thus, informers working Toronto are likely to have just moved from Vancouver and vice versa.

- *Provocateurs:* RCMP informers do not shy from committing crimes in order to gain credibility in an organization, and the political connections of their handlers will ensure no prosecution will result if they do. The result is that they are generally more militant than a group's existing operatives. In 1998, an RCMP informer who had infiltrated a fundamentalist organization in Northern Alberta proved his loyalty by bombing an oil well. It was a better bombing than the existing organization was able to carry off. In hindsight, this made perfect sense since the informant had the resources of the RCMP explosives branch.

In Canada (as elsewhere), there are no absolute guarantees against police informants, and if one rat is going to bring down an organization then the war is already lost. The only insurance is to limit the damage an informant can do by taking fundamental measures such as keeping the various branches and cells of an organization isolated, practicing good housekeeping, and operating on a "need to know" basis. And groups should do everyone a favour by exposing any rats they find. It might discourage others from following their example.

Waging War From Canada
Why Canada is the perfect base for organizing, supporting,
and conducting international insurgency

56

Arms

While the average Mountie, especially in the less-populated provinces, is no different than a kop anywhere, the RCMP does have highly trained paramilitary units. Moreover, they have an excellent relationship with the Canadian military, and are able to borrow equipment, technicians, and advisors — a luxury which would not be available to any other police service. In this respect, the Mounties remain true to their origin as a military organization.

During a recent Indian standoff at Gustafsen Lake, British Columbia, the Mounties showed their military hand. They encircled the rebel camp, laid a perimeter of land mines, and advanced in armoured personnel carriers on loan from the army. They eventually wore down the Indians, who were armed only with hunting rifles, by firing over 9,000 NATO rounds into their camp. It was a military assault no other Canadian police service could have undertaken, one so effective that an American court took the unusual step of allowing one of the activists asylum in the United States on the grounds that he had been persecuted by the Canadian state. There may be a time and a place to get into a fire-fight with the Mounties, but the operative must bear in mind that he will quickly find himself fighting what is essentially a military branch rather than a police force. He should act accordingly.

Mounties are also responsible for protecting Canadian and visiting dignitaries. They rely heavily on false convoys and legions of snipers en route to accomplish this. The result is that low-tech and dirty assaults are often the most successful. In two recent such examples, a member of the Prince Edward Island Pie Brigade (a dadaist insurgency group whose aim is unclear), managed to penetrate a Mountie security cordon and hit the Prime Minister square in the face with a cream pie. Two years ago, an armed schizophrenic managed to wander into the Prime Minister's house and into his bedroom. In spite of all the Mounties on sentry duty around and inside the residence, the country's leader was ultimately protected by his wife and a soapstone Inuit carving. This was an extreme embarrassment to the Mounties, and it is fun to remind them of it whenever the opportunity arises.

It might appear initially that the Mounties are a strong, disciplined, and independent force to be reckoned with. Fortunately, they are not. While they do have great strengths in comparison to other police services, they also have much greater weaknesses. Smart organizations would exploit the latter while avoiding the former.

Political Pressure

The RCMP are the only police service which report to the Government of Canada, and in reality they are directly under the control of the Privy Council and the Prime Minister's Office. This is their Achilles heel, and in effect it means the force will not undertake any operation which is damaging to the Liberal Party of Canada. It will be recalled that the Liberal Party relies largely on the support of immigrants and ethnic minorities — as such, they are very sensitive to accusations of racism. Countless RCMP investigations have been halted on the grounds that they appear to focus on one ethnic group or another. If a terrorist's war is a national liberation struggle in a foreign land, this is his security blanket and perhaps the primary reason why Canada is the best base from which to organize and fund an insurgency. In short, the Mountie dogs can be called off by appealing to the multicultural platitudes of

Waging War From Canada
Why Canada is the perfect base for organizing, supporting,
and conducting international insurgency

58

their political masters. This weakness has been exploited by ethnic groups from all over the world.

A corollary of this is that if a group's fundraising activities are illegal but non-violent (i.e., fraud), they can rely on a certain level of immunity from Mountie persecution by ensuring that a part of their take is channeled to the Liberal Party. In a report by a former Commissioner and 30-year veteran of the Mounties called "The Politicization of the RCMP," Robert Head complains that "heavy political interference exists within the force, particularly on cases involving commercial or 'White Collar' crime." Insurgents should remember who their friends are when times are good and they will return the favour when things get rough. It's the Canadian way.

Because the actions of the Mounties ultimately reflect on the political leader of the country, they are particularly sensitive to failure or criticism. This is especially true in recent years, as a number of Mounties have been convicted of raping young Indian girls. As a result, the force has been softened by government directives to ensure Commanders are women, Francophiles, and minorities; and by expectations that they work on "community policing" and "client relationships," and the quashing of politically damaging investigations. While all of this may make the Mounties a warmer, fuzzier, and nicer force, it also makes them weaker. Their weakness is the terrorist's strength.

Bean Counting

While the Mounties are easily the largest police service in Canada, they also have a lot of ground to cover. Moreover, they are an easy budgetary hit, and they are underfunded to a degree previously unknown in the national police services of most Western nations. This has had a direct effect on what investigations they undertake, and in 1995 a senior investigator made the startling claim that the force would not investigate non-violent crimes where the cost of investigation would exceed the value of assets seized. Careful asset management and a good lawyer will easily be able to ensure that this is the case in the fundraising branch of an insurgent organization.

Money is so tight with the boys in red that in 1999 a major investigation into a nationwide drug smuggling organization was halted on the cusp of success for lack of funding. It was not resumed again until the Province of Ontario agreed to donate six million dollars to resume it, by which time the whole fiasco was public knowledge. The lesson is clear: fighters must make the investigation of their organization as expensive as possible in terms of staff-hours, equipment, expert consultants, and lawyers. Attrition is the key to immunity from the Mounties — insurgents must wear them down, dollar by dollar. At best, they will stop investigating a group's activities altogether as not being cost-effective; at worst, they claim it is not their jurisdiction and fob the job off to a local and less capable service.

The reasons for this state of affairs are many, but in part it is because there is a trend to direct Mountie resources to international efforts which have no effect on activities in Canada. There has been a recent push for the Mounties to dedicate an ever-larger part of their pie to peacekeeping efforts in Cambodia, Haiti, Africa, and the Balkans. The operative should join the clamour to get them out of the country, where they can do no harm. While this draining of resources will have little effect on police presence in the cities, it has an immediate effect if an organization operates out in the countryside. The Alberta crew that recently bombed oil wells for Jesus operated in a sector where there were eight Mounties assigned to police an area of

Waging War From Canada
Why Canada is the perfect base for organizing, supporting,
and conducting international insurgency

60

6,500 square kilometres (about 4,000 square miles). In the end, they got busted because one of their Jesus-freaks was a rat. It came to light, however, that the rat and the bill for the investigation was paid not by the Mounties, but by the targeted oil companies. Praise the Lord and pass the ammunition!

Jurisdiction

One of the main weaknesses of the Mounties is that there are no clear rules for where their jurisdiction lies. In answer to a senate committee question about whether local or national police were responsible for investigating a terrorist attack at the Toronto International Airport, the municipal police said they were responsible unless the attack was "politically motivated," in which case the Mounties were responsible. This sweet stupidity has actually resulted in the Mounties and local police squabbling over jurisdiction — with neither force intervening — during an attack on a foreign embassy. The lesson is clear: terrorists should conduct their operations, where possible, in a manner whereby the Mounties may plausibly deny jurisdiction.

Infiltration

Engaged as they are in more difficult and broader investigations than the junior services, the Mounties rely on civilian informers, academic advisors, and civilian technical consultants to a far greater extent than any other Canadian police force. While this may make them better informed than other police, it also leaves them more open to infiltration. There have been some brilliant examples of this. According to the Mackenzie Institute, a leading Tamil Tiger — using fake Canadian identification — managed to get a job translating documents for an RCMP investigation into the Tamil Tigers. At various times, the force has been infiltrated by Quebec separatists, biker gangs (who got the brass ring of access to PROMIS), and other various comrades. The route is generally to groom candidates to be the perfect applicants for publicly posted civilian jobs or contracts within the force. It's a dangerous game, but if an operative can pull it off he has the enviable ability of deploying state intelligence against itself. He should remember to dress well for the interview — and not use me as a reference.

The Canadian Security Intelligence Service (CSIS)

All of the aforementioned police services are primarily concerned with work-a-day crime taking place on Canadian soil. CSIS, on the other hand, is responsible for investigating espionage and sabotage, foreign-influenced activities, political violence and terrorism, and subversion. In other words, CSIS is the agency most likely to be investigating a terrorist.

That's a good thing. Since its inception in the early 1980s when the RCMP was proving too politically unreliable to handle spooking, CSIS has been a Canadian and international laughing stock. Indeed, their incompetence is one of the main reasons Canada is an excellent place from which to organize operations. Here are a few examples of their many famous exploits:

- *1990:* An audit revealed that the spy agency had lost 833 files. They have never been found.

- *1996:* A CSIS agent left a computer disk containing a list of informants in a public telephone booth. A Canadian

Waging War From Canada
Why Canada is the perfect base for organizing, supporting,
and conducting international insurgency

62

citizen found the disk, booted it up on his computer, and read it. When he realized what he had found, he called the police to arrange its return. An embarrassed and embittered CSIS accused the man who found the disk of being a foreign spy. Editors accused CSIS of being — yet again — hopelessly incompetent.

- *1999:* A high-ranking CSIS agent left a briefcase full of top secret operational plans (which are not, by regulation, permitted to leave headquarters), in her car as she attended a Friday night hockey game. The briefcase was stolen. The agent did not report the theft until she returned to work on Monday morning. The documents were never recovered. It was only one in a long string of leaks, and CSIS vowed to review its document-handling procedures.

- *1999:* CSIS revealed it destroyed the records of informants rather than turn them over to the RCMP, who they did not trust. The feeling was mutual, and the RCMP denied CSIS access to CPIC (the database available to every kop on the street), on the grounds that the spooks are civilians and not police officers. A special committee of the Canadian Senate called the fiasco a "turf battle." This in spite of the fact that both organizations report to the Solicitor General of Canada.

- *2000:* The arrest of Ahmed Ressam, the armed-Islamic group soldier caught trying to smuggle RDX to American millennial celebrations, led to the revelation that CSIS had tracked him for two years. They dropped the surveillance "due to a lack of resources" — without informing the RCMP of his activities.

CSIS agents are not police, they are not armed, and they may not make arrests. Under Canadian law, however, they are allowed greater powers of investigation than kops are. The results of these investigations must be turned over to police for an arrest to be made, but CSIS is reluctant to turn over that information and police are reluctant to trust it. In part, this mistrust is explained by the fact that CSIS tends to recruit from academia rather than police services. The result is that the service lacks "street smarts." Indeed, CSIS lacks credibility even with the Privy Council to whom it reports. This year, the Minister of Finance attended a Tamil Tiger fundraiser against the advice of CSIS. Canada recently established diplomatic relations with North Korea in spite of CSIS urging Privy Council not to on the grounds that North Korean intelligence agents have been actively stealing Canadian nuclear technology and infiltrating public agencies.

Small wonder that morale in CSIS is very low, and the Director of the Mackenzie Institute believes that the best members have sought other employment in recent years. As a result, the quality of their work and reports is surprisingly low — even to the point where their public reports verge on illiteracy. There are about 2,000 full-time CSIS agents with a budget of about 200 million dollars. Recently, they had to transfer soldiers into the service because they were falling years behind on one of their primary duties: security screening of public service recruits. They are not (I know from my many years spent working in the Canadian public service), very good at this.

The one and only publicly known success of CSIS was in the early 1990s, when it managed to place an agent provocateur in the Heritage Front, a rapidly growing neo-nazi organization. It has tried to replicate this success with other groups, but to no avail. In large part this is because CSIS lacks

Waging War From Canada
Why Canada is the perfect base for organizing, supporting,
and conducting international insurgency

64

the ability to recruit informers that the RCMP has. Rather than carefully cultivating, protecting, and rewarding such relationships, the CSIS method of infiltrating ethnic-based organizations is to coerce and threaten refugee claimants into cooperating. Such claimants often cooperate reluctantly, out of fear they will be deported. When they realize that their rights are constitutionally protected, however, or that their claim is accepted, they generally abandon their role as informant or provide the service with misinformation. Recruiting as it does in Canadian universities, CSIS has great difficulty placing agents in groups with particular language or cultural backgrounds. The informants it does place are generally of a very low quality. The intelligence it gathers is mistrusted by the police. CSIS has no credibility with anyone in Canadian society, and it is probably a great comfort to CSIS agents that it is against the law for a Canadian to identify them as such.

Politically directed, riddled with leaks, unarmed, mistrusted by police, embarrassingly incompetent, and lacking all public credibility, CSIS is not a serious threat to an organization if the members take basic precautions to guard against them. In this litany of weaknesses, however, there are two great strengths which fighters must be aware of. Because of their incompetence, CSIS shares all of its information and relies heavily upon the operational assistance of agents from the intelligence services of Canada's allies. This is particularly true in the cases of the United States, Israel, England, and the Commonwealth countries. Canadian citizens pay for this service: in a typical CSIS fiasco, it was recently reported that CSIS was supplying a Mossad hit-squad with Canadian passports. If a terrorist is spooked in Canada, it will likely be a foreign, competent service rather than CSIS.

The second advantage of CSIS is that it enjoys unfettered access to databases held by all level of governments, whereas police services are limited to requesting specific pieces of data. This data includes provincial registries, where key pieces of any false identification will lay. There is an examination of this problem and its solutions in the section on Identification.

The Armed Forces

The Canadian army is small, undernourished, and ill-equipped. During that little dispute with Saddam Hussein (the "Mother of all Battles"), Canada's main contribution was to send a ship to sail safely around the periphery of the Persian Gulf. Even that was delayed until a gun could be dismounted from its perch in a *museum* and fitted to the vessel. Other than that, Canada's main military exploit for the past half century was the Somalian peacekeeping mission, when a platoon of the elite airborne division managed to capture, sodomize, and fatally beat an unarmed 14-year-old "enemy." The airborne division has since been disbanded.

One could go on. The Canadian military is rife with low morale, seriously outdated equipment, and few combat personnel. Next to Iceland and Luxembourg, Canada spends the least on defence of any NATO country. After recent peacekeeping duty in Kosovo, half of the army's armoured equipment was held hostage by the Russian shipping company hired to transport it. The army eventually managed to retake the vessel, but one of the ancient helicopters it used to board it broke down after about a hundred yards' flight and had to return to its launch. Peacekeeping missions to Indonesia were turned back three times because of mechanical problems on Korean War-era transport planes. Once, the planes couldn't even get across lake Ontario — a distance of thirty miles.

Needless to say, foreign powers do not quake in their boots at the thought of a Canadian invasion. Nor does the Canadian

Waging War From Canada
Why Canada is the perfect base for organizing, supporting,
and conducting international insurgency

66

government expect them to. In the mid 1990s, defence policy was dramatically altered. The government faced the fact that Canada could not maintain an army capable of fighting a modern adversary (fuck it — that's what they've got the U.S. for), and concentrated instead on maintaining a lightly armed force to be used for United Nations peacekeeping, propaganda, and domestic deployment.

The usual domestic deployment of the Canadian army is in response to natural disasters: ice storms, floods, and the like that always seem to be landing on Canada. Two years ago, they were even mobilized to shovel the streets of Toronto after a particularly deep snowfall. They are also routinely deployed against illegal fishing trawlers and are often used for domestic search and rescue. This sort of thing is well and good, but what should concern a terrorist operative is not the boy scout work, but rather the "sharp end."

In recent memory, the army has been deployed three times in Canada in a fighting role. Predictably, all three deployments have been against Indians: in 1990 against Mohawks near Montreal, in 1995 at Gustafsen Lake in British Columbia, and also in 1995 at Ipperwash in Ontario. On all three occasions, the army acquitted itself with discipline. On the two latter occasions, hell didn't break loose until the army withdrew and the police moved in.

Short of a national emergency, where the country is put under military rule (as it was in 1971 during the FLQ crisis), an insurgent shouldn't have much problem with the army unless he is breaking into an armoury to get some toys. There are, however, two army organizations every terrorist must be aware of. The first is involved in signals intelligence and the second is involved with counter-terrorism.

Chapter Three
Policing and Intelligence

The Communication Security Establishment (CSE)

The one area of intelligence where Canada has a long history of credibility is in Signals Intelligence (SIGINT). This work began in earnest during WWII, when Canada listened along its long coastlines for enemy submarines. It was perfected during the Cold War, when a number of high-Arctic missile detection stations in the Arctic were complemented by successful efforts at intercepting communications of those nasty Commies who lay just over the North Pole. Canada has developed SIGINT to a high art, and now joyfully deploys it against its own citizens.

The body responsible for domestic SIGINT is the Communication Security Establishment. It is, to say the least, a secretive body. It is also a disciplined one. Unlike CSIS, where leaks to the press are common, only one CSE agent has ever gone public. His revelations, plus testimony given to the Canadian Senate Committee and brief public reports, form most of what is publicly known about the CSE. That may change soon, however, as complaints of low morale and underfunding have begun to leak out of the agency. Whatever the state of the CSE, they cannot hide the huge, heavily guarded antennae and receiving dish complexes which are scattered at strategic places throughout the country.

It is known that the CSE collects electronic communication signals from all sources, even though such collection is illegal in Canada without a search warrant. Public reports of the Civilian Commissioner who theoretically oversees the CSE are simply blunt statements to the effect that the agency has not broken the law. The agency does not answer complaints or inquiries from Canadian citizens, although its Commissioner

Waging War From Canada
Why Canada is the perfect base for organizing, supporting,
and conducting international insurgency

68

may report the findings of any complaint to the Solicitor General, who likewise keeps the findings secret.

In lieu of better knowledge about the CSE, organizations should operate as if the following assertions — all made by credible sources — are fact:

1. The CSE collects all telephonic exchanges and filters them through keyword/pattern detection software for further analysis.

2. The CSE collects all e-mail exchanges and other data sent on Canadian phone lines or radio transmissions and filters them through keyword/pattern detection software for further analysis.

3. Lacking the human resources to conduct analysis of this data, the CSE sends the filtered data to the American Central Intelligence Agency for analysis. The Solicitor General then receives reports of — presumably — whatever the CIA found, wished it found, or wants Canada to think it found.

4. CSE is a "partner" in the American Project Echelon, a worldwide SIGINT network.

Until there is good reason to believe otherwise, every fighting organization in Canada must behave as if all electronic communications are or may be intercepted. If an operative trusts encryption, he should use it even if it is a pain in the ass. If he doesn't trust encryption, he should use other means. He should be careful, especially if his enemy is the United States, as all anecdotes lead to the conclusion that America is the primary beneficiary of Canada's signals intelligence work.

Joint Task Force II (JT-II)

In 1994, responsibility for a military response to terrorism was taken from the RCMP's Special Emergency Response Team (SERT) and given to the armed force's JT-II. Modeled after Britain's Special Air Services (SAS), the unit is reportedly the one combat unit which is well-equipped, well-funded, and in fighting trim. There is no official acknowledgement of the unit's existence, but reliable reports claim they did a good job in Kosovo by getting behind Serb lines to rescue downed pilots and lost scouts, and to laser-sight bombs. They seem to have never been actively deployed in Canada, although that is their primary purpose. This would explain a semi-official complaint that the one thing the JT-II lacks is "experience in Black Ops." Perhaps a terrorist organization could provide them that much-needed experience.

Foreign Spooks in Canada

As long as a fighter is protected by a screen of secrecy, propaganda, and/or political favour, he can likely carry on operations in Canada without undue fear of Canadian police and intelligence services. Certainly many organizations do. In many circumstances, it is more likely that the services he must fear in Canada are those of his homeland or his target. Canada is crawling with foreign spooks, some in cooperation with Canadian authorities and some without their knowledge.

Many foreign spooks are in Canada because it is a safe and useful place to gather intelligence on the Americans without as great a risk of detection. For countries who have diplomatic relations with Canada but not the United States (e.g., Cuba and

Waging War From Canada
Why Canada is the perfect base for organizing, supporting,
and conducting international insurgency

70

North Korea), Canada is the perfect place to transfer American technology. Other state or quasi-state organizations may wish to surveil the United States from Canada so that they may honestly deny operations on American soil. Some of these agents are diplomatic attachés, while others are in deep cover. It was recently discovered that the nice Toronto couple of Ian and Laurie Lambert were really Dimitriy Olshevsky and Yelena Olshevskaya. The cold war may be over, but everyone still wants to keep on eye on the U.S. — and Canada is the perfect place from which to do it.

More relevant to this discussion are foreign agents in Canada for the purpose of gathering intelligence or conducting operations against "terrorists." It has been mentioned that Canada relies heavily on the assistance of foreign intelligence agencies. The closest relationships are with Israel, America, Australia, the United Kingdom, and New Zealand. An operative must assume that any of his activities observed by Canadian Intelligence are also known to the agencies of these countries. It is also likely that it was they who informed CSIS of his activities in the first place, and not the other way around. If there is any comfort in this, it should be that these more threatening agencies cannot work as effectively as they might if confined solely to their own coordination. In assisting Canadian Intelligence on Canadian soil, they are muffled by all the political interference, inefficiency, and incompetence of their junior services — even if they might be sharp and mean on their own terms.

Most dangerous of all are foreign agents working in Canada without knowledge of the Canadian government. They are there because they know the freedom fighter is there. This is particularly true if his cause is national liberation of a foreign country. For every Sikh freedom fighter working underground in Canada, there is bound to be a proportionate Indian

(Calcutta, not Mohawk) agent tracking him. The Tamil Tigers are very active in Canada — and so are the agents of their enemies. Duties range from identifying activists at demonstrations in order to put muscle on kin back home, interception of operational plans, counter-propaganda, and military hits. In one instance, an African national was literally being hunted through the streets of a major Canadian city by a man with diplomatic immunity. In such circumstances, the kops are of no help. He who lives by the sword and all that. It cannot be assumed that allied countries who have agents in Canada at the invitation of the United States do not also have operatives working without Canada's knowledge. This is particularly true of Israel and the United States.

Chapter Four
Raising Money for the Cause

"A further circumstance that has attracted foreign terrorists to Canada has been the ease with which they can raise and transfer funds abroad." — Martin Collacott, Department of Canadian External Affairs

"The problem, of course, is that terrorists don't openly raise funds for explosives or guns but rather for 'humanitarian' purposes, such as education or for orphans." — Steven Emerson, Executive Director, Terrorism Newswire, Inc.

It costs money to wage war. There is no way around it. Even a lone wolf or a small cell requires funds to live off and obtain the limited materiel they require. A national liberation or revolutionary struggle requires endless funds. For a number of reasons, Canada is quite probably the best place in the world from which to raise them. Indeed, a Canadian Senate committee reports that all the world's major insurgency groups (including Columbia's FARC, the Sendero Luminoso, the Khun Sa Militia, the Kurdistan Workers' Party, the Tamil Tigers, and the Hizbi-Islami), all raise funds in Canada through legal

Waging War From Canada
Why Canada is the perfect base for organizing, supporting,
and conducting international insurgency

74

or illegal means. Many groups have found Canada to be such
an effective fundraising ground that they have voluntarily
foresworn any military activity on Canadian soil lest it jeop-
ardize the money train. This suits everybody fine, including
the Canadian government.

Canada is perfectly suited as a base for fundraising. Here's
why:

- *Wealth.* Canada has one of the highest standards of living
  in the world. There is a lot of money there, and the potential to raise a lot of money from Canadians by either legal
  or illegal means. If you want meat, you go to the market.

- *Proximity to the United States.* Besides sharing a long and
  essentially unguarded border, Canada is the largest trading
  partner of the United Snakes of America. It shares the
  same communications infrastructure and finance systems.
  The advantages of this are legion. Legal fundraising
  schemes (i.e., businesses) set up in Canada have access to
  the largest market in the world. Illegal fundraising
  schemes (i.e., drug trafficking, wire-fraud, credit fraud)
  can be conducted against Americans with much less
  chance of getting caught and much less severe penalties
  upon being caught. Moreover, if it is important to an
  operative's cause to be able to deny having "a base of
  operations on American soil," as it is, for example, to
  Hamas, he may technically keep that promise by targeting
  American sources from Canada.

- *Government apathy.* In spite of American pressure to crack
  down on front groups legally raising funds for "terrorist"
  causes, the Canadian government has shown only a token
  interest in interfering. That is because the largest of these
  groups has the presence of mind to keep up appearances

and give a portion of their take to the largest political parties, especially the Liberal Party of Canada. Thus, while the U.S. has the Anti-terrorism and Effective Death Penalty Act to link legal front groups and terrorist organizations, the Canadian Solicitor General has only made a vague commitment to "criminalize" terrorist fundraising at some point in the future. Illegal fundraising is, of course, treated like any other crime, but in the event someone is busted, it is much more difficult for the government to seize the proceeds than it is in most nations. Moreover, the chances of getting caught and the penal sentences for committing such crimes are much less than they are in the U.S.

- *Ease of money laundering.* While the laws and banking practices related to money laundering have recently been tightened (under pressure from the U.S.), Canada still remains a good place from which to launder and move funds. Police have repeatedly complained they have no power to catch money launderers, and there is little political will to change this.

- *Large expatriate communities.* If a fighter's cause is liberation of or a revolution in another country, he will almost certainly find a large number of ex-countrymen living in Canada. Sikh, Somalian, Tamil, Palestinian, and Irish fighters have all, at various times, levied a war-tax on ex-pats living in relative prosperity in Canada. Even without extortion, a sympathetic ex-pat community is likely to be a great source of funds.

- *Easily exploitable Canadian population.* Canadians tend to give generously to national liberation causes if it is presented in a manner that appeals to their naïve little

Waging War From Canada
Why Canada is the perfect base for organizing, supporting,
and conducting international insurgency

76

bleeding hearts. Moreover, there are a number of public income-support causes which can be systematically manipulated to put money in the war chest.

Legal Fundraising

For organizations of scale, the most common means of legal fundraising is to create a front group to which people can donate money under charitable, cultural, or humanitarian auspices. If certain conditions are met, such a front can gain non-profit status — meaning it can raise money without the need to pay taxes or launder money. Organizations with considerable support and manpower can obtain charitable status, meaning Canadians who donate funds to them will not be taxed on those donations. If grown properly, such a front has the added value of serving as a propaganda bureau and a recruiting ground for identifying sympathetic allies and operatives.

Forming a Front Group

If a fundraising front group is to be successful, it must be acceptable to Canadians. If the goal is to buy Kalishnakovs for kids in Chechenya, the stated goal should be to buy artificial limbs for kids who lost their legs to Russian land mines. If the goal is to pay a pension to the wives and children of suicide bombers, the stated goal should be to help widows and orphans. If the goal is to buy a Stinger missile to take down that pesky British chopper, the stated goal should be to promote Irish folk dancing. There is a place for the direct approach to raising funds, but only when soliciting from those already known as sympathizers. If a group wants to operate openly and raise money from as many people as possible, it has to put a nice shine on things. To paraphrase Mary Poppins, "a spoonful of sugar helps the car-bombing go down."

Credibility

It is not enough just to talk about the nice things the group will do with the money it raises — it has to actually do some nice things. And, since any opponents it has in Canada will accuse it of raising money to fund military ops (which, of course, it is), it will need evidence to the contrary. It doesn't have to account for every dollar, or even every tenth dollar, but it does need to be able to credibly argue that its front group is doing the sort of work it claims. The following are the sorts of things which will add credibility to its front:

- *Names, photographs, and narratives of real people who have really been helped by the goup's front.* These must be actual people who will collaborate with the group in the unlikely event they are tracked down by foreign correspondents. If the front purports to educate poor kids, it should put a couple through a university. If the front purports to help children wounded by land mines, it should find a few doe-eyed little brats back in the old country and buy them a peg-leg. To some extent, the front must do what it claims to do, and it must be verifiable.

- *The group must get written endorsements from people not involved in the struggle.* Credible endorsements include those made by church groups working in its homeland, academics, NGO aid workers, and favourable media stories. The gold standard of an endorsement in Canada is one made by a United Nations Human Rights Commis-

Waging War From Canada
Why Canada is the perfect base for organizing, supporting,
and conducting international insurgency

78

sioner. Anything UN is considered God's truth in Canada. Canadians don't realize that most UNHCR's will endorse anything for the price of a hotel room, two whores, and a gram of nose candy. Another excellent source of endorsements, activists, and cash is the Canadian labour movement. The largest and most active private sector union in Canada, the Canadian Auto Workers, have a very busy human rights committee that will get behind anything with a well-spun human rights or class-struggle angle. The umbrella group of all unions in Canada (except, for reasons I won't get into, the CAW) is the Canadian Labour Congress. They also have a human rights committee, but are a little less progressive than their auto-building brethren.

- *The group should use celebrities — even if they are third, fourth, or fifth rate.* The local weather girl can attract more attention, credibility, and money to the front than a thousand earnest pleas. FACT, a Tamil Tiger front in Canada have famous Canadians speak at their fundraisers. Before their unconditional surrender to the Saxons, Provisional IRA fronts in Canada used to be great at drawing people out to their fundraisers by using well-known Irish writers and musicians.

It is likely that the legal front will only be part of the fundraising strategy, and that it will be complemented by extra-legal means such as extortion, smuggling, drug-trafficking, theft, fraud, and counterfeiting. It is vitally important for the credibility and success of the legal front that these strategies remain scrupulously apart. Those involved in the legal front must be respectable citizens or landed immigrants who can never be linked to illegal fundraising activities. Indeed, they must be prepared to denounce and deplore such activities and they must be credible in their denials. This is the Golden Rule of the front organization. To quote a Canadian senate committee, "Fundraising front groups usually take care to commit no crime in Canada. ...drawing a clear connection between funds raised in Canada and a terrorist action elsewhere is often impossible." If someone breaks this rule their front group will be exposed for what it is and they won't get another dime from anyone who doesn't explicitly support their struggle.

A unique exception to the Golden Rule is "the" bad apple strategy which the Provisional IRA once used in Celtic-Canadian non-profit clubs. Local chapters raised money from renting out their hall, bar profits, and holding bog-trotters' balls. These clubs were real — they taught kids Irish dance and so on and they were full of ex-pat Micks reminiscing about the old sod over countless pints of beer. They were governed by a respectable and duly elected board of directors. The treasury swelled. At a certain point, the Treasurer would embezzle all the funds. Once he was safely back in Ireland with the kitty, the other board members would discover his crime. The bad apple would be denounced by the remaining board and to keep up appearances, the police would be asked to make their token investigation. Then the club would mount an ambitious fundraising drive to rebuild its funds. In a few years, the treasury would be embezzled again. Most club members understood the game, but the clubs remained more or less credible fronts because they seriously promoted Irish culture and club members were at least passively sympathetic to the organization behind the front. If Micks — not, let's face it, the sharpest knives in the drawer — can pull this off there's no reason why anyone with a sizable enough émigré population can't do the same. On the other hand, bar profits might not be so high at an Islamic club.

Waging War From Canada
Why Canada is the perfect base for organizing, supporting,
and conducting international insurgency

80

Obtaining Tax-free Status

The ultimate fundraising front is one which operates legally and pays no taxes as a registered charity or charitable foundation. A Canadian Senate Committee looking at the "problem" describes how it works: "Terrorist groups often use benevolent or philanthropic organizations as fronts for fundraising purposes. These benevolent or fundraising groups may even be registered as charities or charitable foundations by Revenue Canada under the Income Tax Act. Such status enhances the credibility of such groups and, ironically, creates the situation where Canadian taxpayers subsidize their activities. People from whom funds are solicited usually have no idea that they will be put to other than legal purposes."

The United States cracked down on this mode of fundraising in 1996 with the Anti-terrorism and Effective Death Penalty Act. Section 302 of that Act allows the Secretary of State to designate "foreign terrorist organizations" to which it is a crime to lend "material support." Since that time, Uncle Sam has been pressuring Canada to adopt a similar law. So far, Canada has resisted. Indeed, our Minister of Finance recently spoke at a FACT fundraiser, a front group of the LTTE which the U.S. has designated as a foreign terrorist organization. It would appear tax-free fundraising will continue to be a valuable option for organizations operating in Canada.

It is a lot of trouble to go through the legal and fiscal tangle of registering a front as a charity or a charitable foundation, and it is not for everyone. For those organizations with the size and resources to do it, however, there are some clear advantages:

- *Legality.* As long as they collect, record, and disperse the money they receive according to the rules, this branch of their fundraising can be squeaky clean. There is no limit to how much can be raised this way and they may send that money overseas with no need to launder it. Moreover, an organization can involve sympathizers in meaningful work who might be shy of getting involved in illegal fundraising or other covert operations.

- *Propaganda.* The very fact of being acknowledged as a benevolent organization by the government of Canada implies that the government endorses their cause. The flip side is that the Government appears to also condemn the cause of their enemy. They may not care what Canada thinks of their cause, but they will like the legitimacy and credibility registration will bring.

- *$$$$$$$.* Once registered as a charity or a charitable foundation, they will find their organization receiving donations from individuals and organizations who might not previously have expressed sympathy to their cause. Their fundraisers can go much further afield. Particularly lucrative are heartfelt appeals to faith groups, union committees, and social justice types. The "charity" should make up some slides of doe-eyed children and show them at every human rights and social justice convention they can find. Obviously, mileage will vary depending on their cause, but for anything that can be framed as a human rights struggle, there is a vast pool of money in Canada. Moreover, registered charities and foundations can issue tax receipts so that donors do not pay income tax on their donations. The effect of this is that individual donations to

Waging War From Canada
Why Canada is the perfect base for organizing, supporting,
and conducting international insurgency

82

registered groups tend to be two or three times as large as
similar donations to unregistered organizations.

Becoming Registered

Becoming registered as a charitable organization is, to be
sure, a complicated undertaking, and it is only suitable for organizations who intend to do long-term fundraising in Canada.
The Canadian government has published a long overview of
the process which untangles the different powers and obliga-
tions of registered charities, private, and public foundations.
No attempt will be made to replicate all that information here,
but it may be found online by going to a search engine such as
www.yahoo.ca, and typing in "Canada Customs and Revenue
Agency," and then searching in the publications section for a
booklet called "Registered Charities and the Income Tax Act."
The whole field is complicated and the details of the Act and
its regulations are in constant flux. There are whole law firms
which specialize in charitable registration in Canada, and a
group will need the services of a lawyer and a certified
accountant to get registered. If the group does not already have
professionals, it should find those with experience working for
front groups rather than "legitimate" charities. The group will
also need unrelated, reliable, respectable, and squeaky-clean
directors to oversee the front organization.

Without bogging down in details, these are the basic requirements for a front to be registered as a charity in Canada:

1. Devote resources to charitable purposes and activities.
    These may be overseas and they may be of a non-partisan
    political nature. Also, donate resources to other charities in
    Canada or abroad. Daisy-chaining such donations makes it

almost impossible to trace what the money was actually spent on. One man's rocket launcher is another man's "medical supplies."

2. Do not pay income to any of the directors or members, except for reasonable expenses or reasonable salaries for employees. Respect this; if people are found skimming cash out of the charity, donations will dry up immediately. Worse, the Government will revoke the front's charitable status. Maintain fiscal discipline and in most circumstances, it must be understood that embezzlers die.

3. Issue official receipts in accordance with the Income Tax Act and regulations. This is a good thing, as it means donors do not have to pay income tax on the money they give. As mentioned above, this fact alone will double or triple the amount of revenue.

4. Keep proper books and records, and make these available for inspection to Canadian tax officials. It is highly advisable that this be handled by a certified accountant. Hire or recruit one who understands the organization and he or she will also prove invaluable in irretrievably concealing the ultimate use of the money raised.

5. File an annual information return on time. This includes the names and addresses of directors and it will be a public document that any Canadian may read. That is why directors must be squeaky clean. The operative no doubt has enemies who will make wild accusations that his group is funding terrorists, and the first thing they will research are the people listed on this return. These people must be as pure as the driven snow. Saints. Virgin saints if possible. No warriors allowed. The success of the front relies on the reputation of its directors.

Waging War From Canada
Why Canada is the perfect base for organizing, supporting,
and conducting international insurgency

84

6. Meet the disbursement quota. In other words, actually spend a specified proportion of the money received on "charitable" works. With the cost of sniper rifles these days, that shouldn't prove difficult.

7. Do not try to meet that quota by exchanging gifts with other charities. This does not mean the front cannot *make* gifts to other charities, just that it can't do it reciprocally to satisfy its disbursement quota. This shouldn't be a problem: the group is bothering with all this bureaucratic crap to win a war, not build a financial empire.

Building Solidarity

The holy grail of legal front groups in Canada is to get Canadians to raise funds for them. The key to this is to build solidarity with wealthy and influential Canadian organizations, including unions, churches, and social groups. For causes that can be framed as leftist, human rights, or anti-racist struggles, this can be remarkably lucrative. For more on this important and often neglected aspect of waging a struggle, see the "propaganda" section of the chapter on Information Warfare.

Extra-Legal Fundraising

Building an effective front requires organization, armies of volunteers, paid professionals, time, and a cause which is at least tolerable to Canadians. Smaller revolutionary organizations, lone wolves, or organizations with misunderstood goals are not likely to have these things. Even many large groups which are capable of creating legal fronts do not wish to for ideological or logistic reasons. In such cases, the cash-starved insurgent has no choice but to turn to his old friend, crime.

Canadian authorities are relatively apathetic about legal war-fundraising, propaganda, and immigration fraud. They are not so keen, however, on crimes committed against Canadians on Canadian soil. If anyone goes about raising funds by any of the means described below, they should expect some degree of police intervention. Go figure. For that reason, it is highly advisable to keep criminal cells separate from the other functional units in Canada and equally separate from each other. One rat or infiltration shouldn't bring down a whole Canadian organization. It's just common sense but it has happened, most notably with neo-fascist groups. With that warning, there are still excellent reasons that extra-legal fundraising can be intensely profitable in Canada. This is especially the case when these activities are conducted against Americans from the safety of a different jurisdiction a few minutes away by car. The following are some extra-legal fundraising techniques that have worked or are working for various groups.

Bank Robbery

You can't talk about extra-legal fundraising without at least mentioning bank robbery. There is an old Provo at a local pub who swears it is the only honourable means of fundraising: Striking twice by buying arms with the enemy's own money. The FLQ in Quebec was also largely financed by bank jobs. But that was a while ago, and things have changed. In Toronto, the average hit-and-run bank job nets a couple of thousand dollars. That might keep a junkie going for a weekend, but it won't do much for a war effort. If a fighter

Waging War From Canada
Why Canada is the perfect base for organizing, supporting,
and conducting international insurgency

86

wants to get at the real money in a modern bank he has got to wait an average of fifteen minutes for the time-release lock. While waiting those fifteen minutes, consider that the average deployment time for police TRU snipers is twelve minutes. Do the math. It can work of course, if the bankrobber is lucky. Sometimes it does. But if he is relying on luck to win his war, he may as well surrender. I suppose a very well-planned bank job, or a very forceful military operation on a bank, has potential. But why bother? There are much easier ways to raise money with much less risk.

That being said, there are sentimental types who think insurgency without armed robbery is like sex without love. For those incurable romantics, a large grocery store is recommended rather than a bank. Talk to someone who closes one on a Saturday afternoon to find out why.

Smuggling

Now we're talking. Consider the following:

- With the exception of marijuana and maple syrup, virtually every commodity in Canada costs much more than it does in America. This includes tobacco, booze, guns, and consumer goods. All of these commodities have ready sellers in America and ready buyers in Canada.

- The Canadian/American border is 4,000 miles long by land. By sea, it includes three oceans, with Alaska, and thousands of miles of freshwater shoreline along the St. Lawrence River and the Great Lakes.

- As this is written, there are exactly 314 American agents policing that border. Almost all of them are concentrated at the major border posts.

Smuggling across the U.S. border has built a number of criminal and insurgent fortunes, and it is so easy that almost all Canadians who live near the border, benefit from it to a greater or lesser degree. Al Capone's empire was built on smuggling booze from Canada to the U.S. The modern Mohawk Warrior Society's empire was built on bringing cigarettes the other way. Whether the cargo is television sets, liquor, BC marijuana, or Chinese immigrants, it is not difficult to get it across the border. How one crosses depends on what is being carried and where. Here are some geographical things to consider:

- *Mohawk territories.* Along the St. Lawrence River and lower Great Lakes (i.e., along upstate New York), there are a number of territories which belong to the semi-self-governing Mohawk Indians. One of these territories (Akwasasne) actually straddles the border. In each of these communities, there are several revolutionary factions, entrepreneurial criminals, and combinations of the two. The politics in these communities are as tangled and fluid as 1950s Sicily, but if an operative can work out an alliance he can pretty much slip across the border at will from the most populated part of Canada to upstate New York. Mohawks are expert river runners and they have a claim to cross-border sovereignty that other Canadians don't have. Moreover, some of them are prepared to back that sovereignty up and they have the arms to do it. Ten years ago, they fought against a planned golf course that would have impinged on their territory. It took the

Waging War From Canada
Why Canada is the perfect base for organizing, supporting,
and conducting international insurgency

88

Canadian army a summer to pin them down, and even then, many of them escaped in a staged riot. Customs on both sides of the border fear these guys. An operative should respect them. If he wants to get into real large scale and sustained smuggling, he should make nice with the Mohawks. That being said, he shouldn't fall into the common trap of thinking there are no Mohawk rats, quislings, collaborators, or plants. Some certainly are. Some are also hardened revolutionaries and many are experienced smugglers. They are likely to be sympathetic to any cause if it involves getting rich or blowing up white guys.

- *The Great Lakes.* Upriver from the Mohawk territories and the St. Lawrence River lie the Great Lakes. These are five freshwater seas, which divide the United States and Canada. The smallest lake (Ontario) is about thirty miles wide and Canada's largest city (Toronto) sits on its Northern shore. During the summer, there are thousands of pleasure boats crossing back and forth, and if you land anywhere on either shore — except in a major port — Customs and Immigration is on the "honour system." Boats are never stopped on the water except when they are committing some obvious marine infraction. This method of smuggling is particularly well suited to smuggling people, as they are self-unloading cargo which can quickly be dumped on the American shore at night and driven off by van. One is unlikely to get caught smuggling on the lakes. On the other hand, one does need a seaworthy vessel and advanced navigation skills. The lakes have their own risks, and their penalties can be greater than any imposed by the Customs man.

- *Main border crossings.* Many smugglers prefer to bite the bullet and cross at a main border crossing, such as Windsor/Detroit. The theory, and it is a sound one, is that there is safety in numbers. Canada has a population of 30 million. There are 110 million border crossings per year between the U.S. and Canada, almost all of them at the major crossings. Most people are only subjected to the briefest interrogation; very few are searched. If soneone is carrying a truckload of cargo this is the only way. As each other's largest trading partners, there are thousands of transports passing back and forth each day at the major crossings; they are much less conspicuous than in the country.

- *Country crossings.* Between the Great Lakes and the Pacific Ocean there are a few major crossings and hundreds of unmarked, intermittently policed country roads. These crossings are fairly risk-free, but they tend to be a long way from anywhere on either side of the border. No cause is worth spending twelve hours in Saskatchewan. The crossings that make the most sense are operating from Vancouver on the Pacific coast. There are large cities on either side of the border (i.e., Vancouver/Seattle), and country crossings in the mountains, not far inland. One should talk to the locals or study aerial photographs available from the Canadian Geographical Survey. This, along with boats on the Pacific Ocean, is the corridor for bringing British Columbia marijuana into the U.S.

Waging War From Canada
Why Canada is the perfect base for organizing, supporting,
and conducting international insurgency

90

Drugs

According to an American Department of Justice report, marijuana grown in British Columbia is five times more potent than Southeast Asian or Mexican. Most concur with this analysis. Everybody loves this shit. The report goes on to say, "Canadian growers are realizing vast profits from their drug exports to this country [estimated at $2-3 billion/year] and little or no effective anti-drug efforts are being undertaken in Canada to combat the problem." Bud is a huge industry in British Columbia and nobody owns it. An insurgent won't have to fight bikers, triads, or the mob to get involved. There's enough for everybody, and it is painfully easy to locate growers on the Canadian side and bulk buyers on the American side.

Cocaine is different. According to the Mackenzie Institute, the Canadian market is largely controlled by the Columbian FARC. It is unclear if that is true, but clearly importation and distribution are much better organized than dealings in marijuana. There is money to be made in Bolivian marching powder, but an operative will have to fight a two-front war to get it. Besides, call me a moralist, but there is something about coke that makes people stupid, greedy, and undisciplined. It can rip an organization apart. At the very least, if dealing in it on any scale a freedom fighter will find himself fighting bikers and other enemies who are more effective and dangerous than the Canadian police.

Counterfeiting and Credit Card Fraud

The American Department of Justice complains that the I-5 corridor (British Columbia-Washington State) "opens opportunities for counterfeiters to operate out of Canada and pass counterfeit checks, currency, and identification throughout the United States." There is nothing special about the I-5 corridor in this respect, and such activities are profitable from anywhere near the border. The financial infrastructure in Canada and the U.S. are completely integrated — a cheque drawn on a Canadian bank can be cashed in an American casino and a credit card issued in Canada is instantly cashed by American merchants. By creating such documents in Canada, however, an operative gains the insulation of passing them in another jurisdiction and, should he get caught, he faces much less prison time than getting caught for the same act in the United States.

There is no need to take counterfeit documents to the United States. Canada is a large enough market to make them rewarding. This is particularly true of forged American currency. While American currency is accepted as legal tender anywhere in Canada (and exchanged at a 1/3 premium over Canadian dollars), most Canadians do not handle a lot of it and will therefore gladly accept poor copies. That, and the fact that American money is much easier to copy than colourful and intricate Canadian cash, makes U.S. counterfeiting in Canada an excellent hobby for the cash-starved insurgent.

In terms of mechanics, counterfeiting, document, and credit card fraud are exactly the same in Canada as they are in the United States. Loompanics Unlimited has many excellent books on the subject, and I will not attempt to synthesize that knowledge here. Suffice it to say that the Mackenzie Institute

Waging War From Canada
Why Canada is the perfect base for organizing, supporting,
and conducting international insurgency

92

is correct when it complains that "credit card fraud and other organized crimes plaguing Canada are sustaining political insurgencies around the globe."

Tele-Fraud

When former United States Attorney General Janet Reno visited Canada recently, her main complaint to the Solicitor General of Canada was the scourge of telemarketing crime. She noted that Canada appears to have a vast number of fraudsters preying on Americans. And they do. The American FBI further reports that over one-half of tele-fraud complaints received are about Canadian telemarketing companies. Not bad for a country of 30 million people.

While lacking the romance of running out of a bank with guns a-blazing, tele-fraud from Canada is really the perfect crime to finance a political struggle. Here's why:

- While it makes purring sounds in response to American pressure, Canada rarely prosecutes persons accused of de-frauding *Americans* by telephone. The onus of such investigations falls on the Americans, and it is notoriously slow and difficult to investigate a crime of this nature in a different national jurisdiction. Even if one ignores all the warning signs and *is* caught, the penalties for tele-fraud in Canada are very light. Canadian courts tend to consider it a victimless crime so long as the victims are American.

- A tele-fraud shop can close in a moment and open the next day at a new location. The only evidence left behind are telephones and party favours.

- It is remarkably lucrative. In one well-known case, a call centre pitching Canadian lottery tickets to Americans raised tens of millions of dollars (the exact amount is unknown, although $12 million was seized) in a matter of weeks. The average age of the mark was 74 years, and their losses ranged from $10,000 to $330,000 each. Small wonder biker gangs, Russian mafia, and Chinese triads have all set up telemarketing shops in Canada as a strong competitor to the comparatively risky businesses of drugs, counterfeiting, and credit card fraud.

- Canada's communication infrastructure and culture is almost completely integrated with that of the U.S. It costs no more to call New Orleans from Montreal than it does to make the same call from New York.

- From a propaganda point of view, if a group is exposed as financing their movement through tele-frauding Americans, you will gain points with general Canadian opinion rather than lose them. Canadians love the idea of pissing off Americans. That is why they yell "Viva Fidel" when Castro visits. If a group is exposed running guns or coke, on the other hand, Canadians may think they are very naughty.

Social Program Fraud

While scaled back in recent years, such programs as welfare, unemployment insurance, workers compensation and student loans still disperse billions of dollars per year. Canada remains a fairly socialist country in comparison to the United States, and a great deal of money flows from the central coffer to individuals. While individual payments are relatively small, a systematic attack on these programs can create a significant source of war funds. For newly arrived groups of immigrants involved in waging war back in the old country, program fraud

Waging War From Canada
Why Canada is the perfect base for organizing, supporting,
and conducting international insurgency

94

is sometimes the only realistic fundraising option. It can be a good option, particularly if the funds are going to a country where the enemy is poor and a Canadian dollar goes a long way.

This is not just theory. The rats at the Mackenzie Institute report that "endemic welfare fraud" forms one of the cornerstones of Tamil Tiger funding. The Institute also reports that Somali warlord (what the hell is a "warlord," anyhow; does anybody know?) Farah Aideed was largely funded by Canadian welfare benefits. These were raised by organizing hundreds of newly arrived Somali refugees to draw several welfare cheques under several different identities. A "tithe" was then drawn on these cheques to Aideed and his crew. Indeed, Aideed's wife and four children lived in Canada and drew welfare benefits, somehow finding the scratch to visit dad in Africa on a regular basis as he attempted to gain support in other African countries.

While public program fraud is a fairly low-risk, low-return funding option for many struggles, it can be committed on a truly heroic scale. A nice Toronto couple recently used Canada's public funding of healthcare to scam $50-100 million using the front of a brick and mortar health clinic. As this is written they are on a luxury yacht somewhere on the Eastern seaboard, hoping to make it to Panama, which has no extradition treaty with Canada. Happy sailing, kids. Some Ghanaian operators exploited Canada's student loan program by dressing up a few rented offices as a "post-secondary training institute" and obtaining loans for thousands of fictional students. They made off with approximately $50 million. Both of these episodes were purely criminal rather than insurgent fundraising, but it shows the potential.

Public program fraud is low risk — it's something almost every Canadian does at some level — but if done on a large scale, the gig will eventually be revealed. One must hit quick, obfuscate the paper trail, and make sure whoever takes the blame is out of the country when the books are finally tallied. If the Canadian government won't stand up in the United Nations and support a group's cause, the group can at least have the satisfaction of letting them pay for it.

Money Laundering

If relying on extra-legal fundraising techniques, whether it be smuggling, fraud, drug dealing, extortion, or any other method his evil little mind can conceive of, the terrorist is left with a problem. Most, if not all, of his revenue will be cash. How does he use, protect, and move this money? In other words, how does he launder it? There is nothing more dangerous, revealing, or subject to seizure and factional infighting than a trailer-load of twenties.

Not long ago, Canada was a well-known haven for money launderers. Haiti's Baby Doc brought his cash there, as did the New York Cosa Nostra. The Americans didn't like Canada's attitude, and under intense pressure the Canadian laws have recently been tightened. The thousand-dollar bill, for example, was discontinued, and financial institutions are now theoretically obliged to report "suspicious" transactions to the RCMP. The insurgent need not be scared by this, though. A lot of political campaigns are supported by money laundering and it supports a goodly number of law firms. Attempts to crack down on it are largely a matter of form. This is revealed in the transfer of one of the RCMP's detachment commanders — a leading expert in tracing "proceeds of crime" — to a remote corner of rural Alberta. Canada is still a good place from which to launder money. Not as good as, say, the Cayman Islands, but still much better than the United States.

Waging War From Canada
Why Canada is the perfect base for organizing, supporting,
and conducting international insurgency

96

According to a helpful pamphlet published by the Royal
Canadian Mounted Police, there are very good reasons to
launder excess cash:

"Avoid prosecution, increase profits, avoid seizure of accumulated wealth, appear legitimate, [and] tax evasion. The
principal objective of money laundering is to convert cash to
some other form of asset, in order to conceal the illegal source
or origin of cash income. Criminals eventually use these
funds, ascribed to a 'legitimate' source, which then cover the
tracks of the illegitimate business that generated the cash in
the first place."

When the LTTE posed as the Bangladesh army to purchase
60 tonnes of Ukranian military-grade explosives, they used
their Canadian accounts to pay for it. That transfer — and the
ruse behind it — would not have been possible, except that the
money had already been legitimized in Canada.

Methods of Money Laundering in Canada

As with charitable registration, there are many lawyers who
specialize in money laundering and little else. If the intention
is to legitimize money on a large or ongoing scale, it is good
to procure the services of one of these land-sharks. Some of
them have their own teams of couriers and smurfs — who
have no knowledge of whose money they are cleaning. Moreover, the lawyers themselves — who work for a fixed percent-
age of the total money laundered — are completely reliable.
They have more to lose than the insurgent, since if the jig is up
they will not only face the wrath of his organization, but they
will lose the right to practice law. They may also go to jail,
where they will be the butt of constant jokes about what fine
lawyers they are.

Actually recommending any of these lawyers in print would just be stupid. It is not hard to locate them, however. They tend to have web sites, often catered toward an Asian clientele. They tend to use words like "careful," "reliable," and "discreet" to describe their practice. They also tend to describe their services as "offshore investments." If an organization does not already have a lawyer, it can just arrange a meeting with one of these lawyers and ask him or her straight up. The worst they can say is "no," and the conversation is protected under client-lawyer privilege. Alternately, the group can just do the job itself.

The following are the chief methods of money laundering in Canada:

- *Smurfing.* This is the most common method in both Canada and the United States. It involves hiring a number of "smurfs" to travel around making small cash deposits in various bank accounts. The only reason this works better in Canada than in America is that the Canadian threshold where banks must report cash deposits is higher: $10,000.

- *Currency exchanges.* These helpful agencies will exchange Canadian money for foreign currency, which may then be smuggled out of the country. They can also wire money to offshore accounts.

- *Securities brokers.* Some stockbrokers will exchange securities for cash on a large scale without reporting it.

- *Assets.* Operatives and allies may be paid with goods rather than money.

- *Travel agencies.* People in an insurgent organization probably like to travel a lot. Why not exchange cash for airline tickets?

Waging War From Canada
Why Canada is the perfect base for organizing, supporting,
and conducting international insurgency

98

- *Credit cards.* A high over-balance can be redeemed any time, anywhere.

- *Casinos.* Cash can be refined to cashier's cheques.

- *Refining.* Smurfing small bills to larger dominations. This is why the Canadian mint recently stopped printing the Canadian $1,000 bill — it was a favourite of refiners everywhere.

- *Co-mingling of funds.* This is the sophisticated end: investing in legitimate cash-transaction businesses such as restaurants and mixing the dirty money with the clean.

- *Reverse flip.* A launderer buys undervalued real estate and pays the difference in cash. After a time, the property is sold for its real value, legitimizing the difference.

The RCMP is the main police body responsible for investigating money laundering in Canada. They have repeatedly complained that they have neither the staff, the resources, nor the expertise to do much about it. They also complain that many of their investigations are thwarted by political interference from the Privy Council. Convictions are extremely rare.

Chapter Five
Information Warfare

"Louis J. Freeh, Director of the United States Federal Bureau of Investigation, has characterized Canada as a 'hacker haven'..." — Canadian Senate Committee

Information warfare has come to be associated with the cracking and sabotage of computer data, applications, and networks, but it has a much richer history than that. Data encryption was an important intelligence activity long before Bill Gates was daddy's little bitstream, and the cutting of telegraph wires and the scuttling of dispatch ships had the same aim as modern denial of service attacks: confuse the enemy's communications. That being said, the Internet and the desktop PC are supposed to have democratized the means of information warfare. For reasons I will go into below, I don't believe that substantial harm can be done to the enemy — from Canada or elsewhere — through computer networks. There is a lot of hype surrounding cyber-war. Nevertheless, when choosing to wage cyber-attacks on targets, Canada is an excellent place from which to launch them. A more effective use of computer

Waging War From Canada
Why Canada is the perfect base for organizing, supporting,
and conducting international insurgency

100

and networking technology is to gain imagery and background intelligence. In other words, the Internet does not present new opportunities for warriors so much as it aids traditional means of intelligence gathering and communications warfare. The most effective form of information warfare remains the ancient art of propaganda. Canadians, bless their naïve little souls, are suckers for propaganda and are happy to carry it to the United Nations by the truckload.

Internet/Network Attacks

A number of Internet attacks have been launched from networked computers in Canada. Most of them, as with attacks launched from elsewhere, were of the web site defacing variety. While it may be fun to paste swastikas on the American Department of Justice web site, it doesn't really impede their work. Some geek just has to grab the HTML code off of a backup tape, reload it, and fine-tune the firewall. Big deal. Don't consider this sort of attack to be of any serious consequence, and even from a propaganda perspective, it is of extremely limited value. Defacing web sites is not warfare. It is wanking.

More important are cracks which have economic consequences. A well-intentioned Canadian kid has been a star of the Canadian press lately (although under Canadian law, he can't be identified except by his computer nickname of "mafia-boy") for launching denial of service attacks on the web sites of CNN, e-bay, and a number of other prominent American web sites. His motives seem to be those of a youthful prankster rather than a soldier, but teams of FBI agents were flown up to Canada to help inept Mounties bust the lad. This they did, and by the tone of their press releases you would think they had just caught Osama bin Laden. Ridiculous estimates claimed that the few hours of disruption the boy caused the American economy amounted to hundreds of millions or even billions of dollars. So what? A million "mafia-boys" could spend all day fucking up the web sites of American corporations and the effect on the American economy would be negligible. The same is true of any other country, and unless the target is specifically a corporation that operates on the web, such attacks are a mug's game.

There are, of course, exceptions. Credit card and banking information has been cracked from web sites to fund criminal and possibly insurgent organizations. Likewise, a Canadian criminal organization recently cracked an online insurance database to find out the car license number of a troublesome reporter, whom they then shot five times in the back. The Internet can be a valid place to gain or spread information, but it is very rare that it can be used to actively damage the enemy.

Look at the evidence. Probably the most famous military network hack in the world was Marcus Hess's ring gaining access to fifty military computers at the Pentagon, Los Alamos, and various defense contractors. While it made big news, the fact is that none of the information obtained by these hacks — or the 160,000 other successful penetrations per year into Pentagon computers — was classified. The simple fact is that "mission-critical" information is held on networks which are stand-alone. In other words, the data that can really harm an enemy is sealed in networks unconnected to the Internet and with no dial-in access. A worldwide effort to cyber-attack East Timor was embarrassingly ineffective for this reason alone. Cracking mission-critical networks and databases can only be done from the inside. While not impossible, this is a much more daunting proposition than hacking a web site.

Waging War From Canada
Why Canada is the perfect base for organizing, supporting,
and conducting international insurgency

A Canadian Senate Committee concluded that "the Internet provides an unprecedented security threat," but they are just caught up in the hype. There are only two known exceptions where truly mission-critical information was hacked over telephone lines. Both were launched from Canada. In one case, top-secret information was downloaded from India's Bhabha Atomic Research Centre. In another instance, a satellite operated by the People's Republic of China was disabled. Both of these successful attacks have a common denominator: they were launched on countries with technical savvy but, in general, old communications and networking technology. Most countries which rely on communications technology to any degree have set out on a deliberate program of isolating, or "hardening," mission-critical networks. The United States and Europe are at the forefront of this strategy. Anyone who thinks they are going to shut down the power grid of New York with a modem is dreaming.

There are those who disagree on the utility of hack-attacks, and who think remote technical attacks have potential to damage the enemy. The following are reasons, then, why those people should choose Canada from which to make their misguided attacks:

- *Infrastructure.* A recent study has found that Canadians use the Internet and personal computers in general more than any other population on earth. Similarly, Canadian government documents and businesses can be accessed over the Internet more readily than any other country. As this suggests, communications infrastructure is well advanced. Even remote communities have fiber-optic backbones and DSL or cable connections. More importantly, this infrastructure is completely unified with American infrastructure, making it easier to "spoof" the origin of an attack. Should the target be American, one would have all the access of a Yankee while being remote in terms of legal jurisdiction.

- *Law.* No serious information attack has ever been made against a Canadian network, and as a result, there has been no push to harden the law against such attacks. While America and most European countries have specifically criminalized cyber-attacks, in Canada they fall under the catch-all section of the Criminal Code for "Mischief." Unless the mischief directly endangers life, the penalties are not serious. A person attacking American or other foreign networks from Canada would be tried — if caught — under Canadian law. Such a person could not be extradited if the attack originated in Canada. In other words, even if someone does get caught, he will get off easy. The relevant section of the Criminal Code (430) reads as follows:

(1.1) Anyone commits "mischief" who willfully

- destroys or alters data

- renders data meaningless, useless, or ineffective

- obstructs, interrupts, or interferes with any person in the lawful use of data

- denies access of data to any person who is entitled to access thereto.

- *Enforcement.* Fortunately, Canadian koppers have little capability to investigate cyber-attacks. According to the national press, the RCMP detachment responsible for Canada's nearest equivalent to Silicon Valley has nine officers

Waging War From Canada
Why Canada is the perfect base for organizing, supporting,
and conducting international insurgency

104

who could "potentially" deal with computer crime. Of those nine, two have training in the area. The other seven are probably taking courses in Word97 and figuring out how to use Netscape. Contrast this to the American Federal Computer Emergency Response Team (FedCERT), and its National Infrastructure Protection Center — they have the ability, the knowledge, and the resources to instantly respond to cyber-attacks.

Intelligence Gathering

While arguably useless as a weapon, the Internet is undoubtedly a useful resource for intelligence gathering. Sites such as mapquest.com provide detailed street maps of municipalities and organizations publish detailed plans and images of potential targets. Appearances of legitimate targets at business, academic, and diplomatic conferences are published on the web sites of the organization hosting those meetings. A lot of useful intelligence about the enemy can be garnered through creative use of the Internet, but there is nothing special about Canada in this respect — except, perhaps, that Canada tends to have higher connection speeds than the rest of the world.

Propaganda

The oldest and most important form of information warfare for the insurgent or revolutionary is propaganda. A Canadian Senate Committee complained that every terrorist organization or front group maintains a web site to disseminate propaganda, but the Internet is just one small adjunct. Most terrorist organizations can never hope to overwhelm their enemies by sheer military might. Propaganda is likely to be their greatest weapon. As such, it cannot be limited to a web site. Everything must be propaganda: every refugee claim, every appearance of leaders and organizers, every trial, and every pitch for funds. Every military action must be weighed against its propaganda in terms of value or harm.

Canadians, as will be shown, are particularly vulnerable to certain types of propaganda. If an organization is operating in Canada, there are good reasons to win Canadian hearts and minds, even if Canada is incidental to the cause.

Protection

As has been noted, the authority for Canadian policing and intelligence ultimately lies with the Privy Council, which is directed by senior elected politicians. There is no non-partisan body such as the American Central Intelligence Agency between the politicians and the agents. The result is that Canadian kops and spooks are indirectly held hostage to the political pressures of their masters.

Well-organized movements will take advantage of this weakness in the Canadian system. A good example was the attempted deportation of Manickavasamagam Suresh, a key Tamil Tiger fundraiser, in 1996. When the immigration office seized him and began deportation proceedings, the Tigers mobilized some 25,000 protestors. They mainly targeted Toronto-area cabinet ministers — those with direct influence on the Privy Council. The result was that Mr. Suresh was released and allowed to stay in Canada to continue fighting the good fight. The politicians, in short, could not withstand the Tamil

Waging War From Canada
Why Canada is the perfect base for organizing, supporting,
and conducting international insurgency

106

propaganda, and as they buckled, so did the kops who answered to them.

Credibility

Canada is at best a middle power, but it has more sway in the United Nations and other international bodies than its population, its economy, or its strength would imply. International engagement has been, for the past half-century, the overriding theme of Canadian foreign policy. This internationalism is a two-edged sword in the hands of insurgents. On one edge, Canada's respected and impartial voice in support of a cause can lend it legitimacy in the international community. On the other edge, Canada itself is overly sensitive of criticism from that community, and will go to great lengths to prevent embarrassment.

Except in very rare instances — such as the recent Canadian condemnation of Israel at the United Nations — Canada will not take a cause directly to international forums. It can be made to appear to support a cause, however, even without such direct intervention. A common means of using the Canadian government to add international legitimacy to a cause is through the use of staged refugee claims.

As previously noted, almost anyone arriving in Canada has the right to claim refugee status. Many organizations — Northern Irish, Israeli, and even American — have sent operatives to make politically charged claims which, while unlikely to succeed, add credibility by virtue of the fact that they are heard and publicly reported upon. The value of such claims cannot be underestimated. Israeli-Canadian diplomatic relations were severely weakened in the 1990s when Israel objected to Canada's hearing of a number of Israeli refugee claims. This in spite of the fact that, under Canadian law and

International Agreement, Canada had no choice but to hear them. In an interesting mirror image of this process, a Canadian Indian activist recently embarrassed Canada by claiming — and receiving — political asylum in the United States. Refugee claims are but one example of using Canada to gain international credibility. Every international academic forum, standards body, diplomatic conference, cultural event, and business meeting is a chance to spread propaganda. Merely attending these meetings adds credibility and implicit recognition to a movement. Often, they present an opportunity to hijack the agenda and force representatives of an insurgent's enemy into defensive positions. At other times, they present an opportunity to inspire others with the justice of a cause. Not all soldiers carry a rifle — some must carry a briefcase and a Palm-Pilot. Others must carry a guitar and a microphone. Many groups, such as the LTTE, the Zapatistas, and the Iranian Communist Party deliberately use publicly owned spaces for their fundraising and commemorative events. The use of public spaces, which would never be opened to "unacceptable" groups such as neo-nazis, implies community consent in the credibility of their cause.

Fundraising

If one wishes to see Canadian funds directed to a front organization, it is necessary to build up knowledge of and sympathy for one's struggle among Canadians. This subject has already been touched upon in Chapter Four, but it bears repeating that fundraising and propaganda are parts of the same thing. Fundraising activities are propaganda activities, and good propaganda will generate funds. An excellent example of this is the Zapatista movement in Southern Mexico,

Waging War From Canada
Why Canada is the perfect base for organizing, supporting,
and conducting international insurgency

108

which raised money and sympathy at the same time through benefit concerts — which became weekend fixtures for the Canadian urban left.

Propaganda Strategy in Canada

Propaganda efforts will necessarily be targeted toward those directly affected by and involved in a struggle. Depending on the nature of the war, these will be immigrants from the old country who now live in Canada, people who share a similar religion or sect, or those who share a similar political or social ideology. In other words, it is necessary to preach to the converted or those who ought to be. In order to milk the rich value of propaganda for protection, credibility, and funds in Canada, however, it is necessary to take the propaganda to the wider Canadian society.

Organizations that have succeeded in Canadian propaganda efforts have done so largely because they have understood their audience. They have written off the majority of Canadians — the great mass of sheep who merely dedicate their lives to grazing and defecating — as having no value. They have instead concentrated their fire on what historians call "the political nation."

The political nation is comprised of those who have a direct or indirect influence on political or otherwise powerful institutions. It includes those who wield political power, such as members of parliament, but also includes those who shape the policies of those in power (e.g., political staff, bureaucrats, journalists, academics, business people). It also includes those who exert a moral force over public policy (e.g., clergy, artists). Equally important, it includes those who are politically engaged from the outside (e.g., trade unions, fringe parties, social activists). Together, this nation is the target of effective propaganda.

While politically engaged, only a small minority of the Canadian political nation will be interested in any narrow liberation or ideological struggle. It is therefore necessary to widen the scope of a struggle to make it appeal to a large section of the Canadian political nation. While widely divergent, this nation shares some common values: it is "progressive" and "liberal" in the broadest sense; it has no taste for racism; it likes to see itself as compassionate and committed to human rights. To appeal broadly to this nation, propaganda must speak to the broader sentiments of the political nation rather than the narrow confines of a particular struggle.

A good example of this precept in action was during the upheaval in Somalia. Khagida Gurkhan, the wife of Mohammed Farah Aideed, a Somalian "warlord," had claimed Canadian refugee status and was actively fundraising for her cause in Canada. Few non-Somalians knew or cared about her small struggle in an unimportant country, and she was criticized by some media for apparently levying a war-tax among Somalian refugees. Rather than attempt to justify the cause of her husband's faction, Gurkhan labelled the attacks as racist. She solicited the aid of the Black Action Defence Committee — a Canadian civil rights group — and other social activists. The media criticism stopped and there were none of the police proceedings which, until that time, appeared inevitable.

A more active stance can be effective so long as it is in keeping with the precepts of the Canadian political nation. In the late nineties, various Kurdish front groups were having a hard time in Canada — they were, for whatever reason, subjected to more police harassment than other similar groups. When police arrested "terrorist leader" Abdullah Ocalan, the Kurds struck back. Claiming human rights violations, they or-

Waging War From Canada
Why Canada is the perfect base for organizing, supporting, and conducting international insurgency

110

ganized riots in Ottawa and Montreal, largely endorsed by Canadian activists and radicals who were engaged — if only negatively — in Canadian policy. These were harder actions than Canadians were used to seeing: one kop lost an eye (justice is blind), and another was set on fire with a Molotov cocktail. Still, the staged riots were effective, and Kurdish fronts were henceforth able to operate without undue scrutiny. Contrast this to similar riots waged by Serbian-Canadians over Canadian participation in NATO raids. The Serbs did not attempt to link their struggle to any wider value or appeal to the Canadian political nation. As a result, their riots — while as hard as the Kurdish riots — had no effect whatsoever. If anything, they merely confirmed the Canadian perception of Serbs as being unstable and somewhat creepy.

A corollary of all this is that there are some causes for which propaganda is detrimental. These are causes which run contrary to the shared values of the Canadian political nation. Such things include white-power, anti-Semitic, and neo-nazi organizations. Any propaganda waged by such groups might reach the ears of sympathetic Canadians, but they will be Canadians who do not matter. The propaganda of such groups cannot be spun in a way as to be acceptable to the political nation, and any such propaganda will do more harm than good as far as protection, credibility, or funding is concerned. It must be kept in mind that, in comparison to the United States, there is only a very limited right to free speech in Canada. If the propaganda runs too counter to the precepts of the political nation, that organization will find the whole weight of that nation bearing down upon it. This is what happened to German and American neo-nazi groups operating in Canada in the 1990s: their propagandists were charged with "hate crimes," their non-citizen activists were deported; their books carefully audited; and, their ranks were heavily infiltrated by police.

More recently, a sixteen-year-old was jailed for writing third-person fiction in which the hero of the story bombs his school. This Stalinist persecution would be unacceptable for organizations able to spin their cause as somehow being related to human rights. If one is a member of a racist or far-right group, the best propaganda in Canada is silence. Preach only to the converted. Better yet, follow your leader by building a bunker and then shooting yourself in it.

Chapter Six
Military Operations

"We have noticed a disturbing trend as terrorists move from significant support roles, such as fundraising and procurement, to actually planning and preparing terrorist acts from Canadian territory." — Canadian Security and Intelligence Service

"The United States government considers that... Canada could be a conduit for transporting nuclear, biological, or chemical materials into the United States, or could be a venue for planning a nuclear, biological, or chemical attack against the United States." — Canadian Senate Committee

The thing that generally distinguishes "terrorist" organizations from lobby groups, protest movements, and opposition parties is the belief that violence is required to further their cause. And sometimes, of course, it is. There would be no State of Israel had Ben Gurion not been willing to hang British soldiers. There would be no Palestine had Arafat not adopted the same philosophy. Without an active military opposition,

Waging War From Canada
Why Canada is the perfect base for organizing, supporting,
and conducting international insurgency

114

South Africa would still have its homelands and Germany would still have its camps. But there's no need to convince you of that; if you've read this far you are already convinced that somebody has got to lose an eye. While Canada is most often used by insurgents as a base for organizing, fundraising, intelligence gathering, and propaganda, it can also be the sharp end.

Targets in Canada

If a military target is American or an organization or individual is American, the advantages of operations basing in Canada are obvious. It is the only country bordering the continental U.S. except for heavily guarded Mexico. Even if the target is Asian, African, Middle Eastern, or European, Canada may still be a good place to conduct a military operation. Canadian institutions attempt to remain internationally engaged, and there are hundreds of political, academic, military, diplomatic, and business conferences at which targets from all over the world may appear. Moreover, given the apparent peacefulness and disarmament of Canada, such targets are certain to appear far more publicly and vulnerably than they would back in the old country.

The Dominion of Canada was founded in response to Fenian (Irish nationalist) raiders from the United States attacking Canada because it was a softer target than England itself. That logic was good in 1867 and it remains good today. It was the same logic used in a recent attempt to bomb the Israeli embassy in Quebec, which was only thwarted when Tarek Khafagy (a Hezbollah operative) was ratted out by the relative who bought the explosives. While rare, there have been some stunningly successful military operations conducted in Canada, including:

- *Kidnappings:* The most famous terrorist kidnapping in Canada was the FLQ seizing of James Cross, a British diplomat. More recently, Hezbollah operatives in Montreal kidnapped a woman to inspire her Egyptian boyfriend to follow orders.

- *Bombings:* In 1985, Sihk warriors organized, procured, and planted a bomb on Air India 182 at the Toronto International Airport. Three hundred and twenty-nine people were killed. The RCMP have been diligently charging, interrogating, and surveilling suspects ever since, but so far there have been no convictions. While Canadian airport security was somewhat bolstered, it still remains softer than that of most countries.

- *Assaults:* In 1985, Armenian warriors were successful in a military assault and occupation of the Turkish embassy in Canada.

- *Assassinations:* In the mid-1990s, a number of rival Tamil factions made hits on each other until an LTTE commander came over from Sri Lanka to make peace. The most famous political assassination in Canada was the execution of Pierre Laporte (Quebec Minister of Labour) by French nationalists. More recently, Sikh assassins hit a reporter whom they had found guilty of publishing counter-propaganda.

The fact that diplomatic targets are softer in Canada than they are back in the old country emerged during a public inquiry into RCMP incompetence at a recent APEC conference held in Vancouver, British Columbia. In the sea of official

Waging War From Canada
Why Canada is the perfect base for organizing, supporting,
and conducting international insurgency

116

memos which were made public as a result of the inquiry, a few jewels were exposed. One was that (the then) president of Indonesia Suharto was concerned about the ability of Canadian police to protect his security. The reason for his concern was that Canada would not allow his bodyguards to carry weapons. During the inquiry, it was revealed that Canada does not allow *any* foreign emissary or bodyguard to carry arms, with the sole exception of American FBI Special Service agents protecting the President. Fire at will.

As an exemplary Canadian, I should mention here that an insurgent group must carefully weigh the benefits of conducting military strikes in Canada. They will be certain to destroy the beneficial effects of any propaganda, and they will call a lot of undue attention to their organization. They may also endanger the rest of us. The United States has been pressuring Canada for years to make Canada a less terrorist-friendly country, and too many domestic attacks will force them to fold under that pressure. Still, there have been organizations that have concluded that military operations in Canada were necessary or justified. Many more have concluded that it is an excellent base from which to purchase, store, build, or ship weapons.

American Targets

Organizations seeking to strike at Uncle Sam will find clear advantages to organizing and launching military attacks from Canadian soil. Some of those advantages are:

- *Jurisdiction.* Assuming one survives an attack on the Great Satan, it is better to get to another national jurisdiction until the heat dies down. An investigation will be much more difficult for the FBI across a national border, and even if someone is busted, there will be a long process of appealing extradition orders. Moreover, Canada has no barbaric death penalty and will not generally extradite people likely to face it. For all these reasons, the New York World Trade Center bombers intended to flee to Canada when their work was done, where they had already established false identities. They got caught before they made the border. Better luck next time. Similarly, Mohawk warriors who shot down a U.S. National Guard helicopter in 1990 could never have survived except that they were able to retreat across the border where other Yankee choppers couldn't pursue.

- *Ease of transport.* As noted earlier, the Canadian/U.S. border is 4,000 miles long and protected by 300 American border control agents. It is much easier to transport arms and soldiers into the United States from Canada than it is from any other country. Much easier. It was only poor planning and bad luck that allowed the 1999 border interception of the Algerian soldier carrying 50 kilograms (100 pounds) of RDX in his car, or the 1995 capture of the American white supremacist smuggling 130 grams of Ricin, a nasty biological agent. As presented to a United States Senate Committee on northern border security, "terrorists, and also illegal aliens, alien smugglers, and drug smugglers, are increasingly using Canada as a transit country en route to the United States."

- *Lack of surveillance.* Military activities and individual soldiers operating in Canada are much less likely to come under official surveillance in Canada than in the United States. The American militia movement, for example, while not active or particularly popular in Canada, has

Waging War From Canada
Why Canada is the perfect base for organizing, supporting,
and conducting international insurgency

118

nevertheless used Canadian rural areas for arms dumps and training fields. It was this lack of surveillance which led Hani al-Sayegh, one of the Hezbollah responsible for the 1996 Saudi bombing which killed 19 U.S. soldiers, to come to Canada after the job was done. He enrolled in a university, and by all accounts was a good student. Ultimately, his undoing was American rather than Canadian intelligence.

Many American targets can be hit without even leaving the relative safety of Canada. Most Canadian industries are branches of American corporations — the exception being American businesses, consulates, and missions, and their personnel are much less guarded and armored in Canada than in most countries. The day after the bombing of the American embassy in Kenya, I asked a friend who owns a one-ton panel van to park it in front of the University Avenue American Consulate in Toronto, just to see what would happen. Nothing happened, and it became clear during a Serbian-Canadian riot at the same location that the windows were merely plain window glass. Many leading American politicians and their senior staff vacation in Canadian hunting/fishing camps that they own or rent. They come every year, at the same time of year, to the same place. I worry about their safety.

In an interesting counter-example, in 1985, Armenian terrorists pissed off at Canada's support of allied Turkey bombed an Air Canada office in Los Angeles. What's good for the goose is good for the gander, right?

Military Supply

While military assaults are occasionally made in Canada, they are rare. It is, after all, a peaceful country. That is one of the main reasons that Canada is such an excellent base of operations. Much more prevalent than actual assaults is that other essential element of military operations: supply.

Explosives

Canada's economy is based on natural resources, and they often have to be blown, blasted, and exploded. There are a lot of explosives in Canada and they are less controlled than in America or, for that matter, almost any other country.

Ah, explosives. If I may wax sentimental for a moment, I would like to relate a story from my youth. After ramming our way into an isolated and unguarded mining explosives shack in British Columbia when I was about 19, my mates and I spent a wonderful summer blowing up hydro pylons, small bridges, and a local business that required a lesson in customer service. Bombs are an important military tool, of course, but they are also a lot of fun. All work and no play makes Mohammed a dull holy warrior. But I digress.

At one time, reliable information on making explosives was only disseminated in chemistry books and by disreputable publishers. With the Internet, of course, that has all changed. Now even the most under-financed lone wolf can find all sorts of interesting recipes. Results may vary, however. The best-known home-brew ingredient is ammonium nitrate, which is available in commercial fertilizers. Supposedly, American manufacturers of fertilizer place microscopic plastic tracers in their wares so the source and approximate date of procurement may be forensically determined. This may be true; however some good sources say that Canadian fertilizer producers use no such tracer.

For more sophisticated organizations, homemade solutions won't do. That requires commercial or military grade explo-

Waging War From Canada
Why Canada is the perfect base for organizing, supporting,
and conducting international insurgency

120

sives. A licence to obtain commercial explosives may be easily obtained by enrolling one of a group's operatives in a short
certification course. Better yet, such explosives may be stolen
from one of thousands of construction and mining depots. The
credibility of Canadian accounts and/or shell-companies will
allow the organization to purchase explosives in bulk from
Eastern European manufacturers. The LTTE used Canadian
accounts to purchase a cargo-ship full of Ukranian TNT and
RDX — a purchase that went a long way to ensuring the inevitable success of their struggle. Perhaps other organizations
should save their pennies and do the same.

Components and Dual-use Agents

As Amerika's largest trading partner and trusted ally, Canadian institutions have open access to virtually all biological
and chemical agents produced there as well as the relevant
technologies. Yet, the laws and practices controlling the sale
and shipment of these products are much less strict in Canada
than in the U.S. As a result, many organizations have established procurement and shipping networks in Canada to obtain
material which might be prohibited or tightly controlled in the
U.S. or abroad. This is particularly true in the case of "dual-
use" chemical and biological agents which have both civilian
and military utility. Some of these might even be used by sophisticated and well-funded organizations to produce weapons
of mass destruction.

Recent top-secret CSIS memos exposed by Canadian media
revealed that many organizations operate in Canada for the
sole purpose of obtaining these products. According to these
reports, several organizations have established "clandestine
procurement networks" using front companies and "deceptive

shipping practices" to obtain dual-use agents. A typical example was an Iranian "researcher" requesting a Canadian toxicologist to provide a fungus which produces a powerful toxin. The memos noted sixty-one such unsuccessful attempts at obtaining material and imply that the vast majority of such attempts succeed.

As important as components and agents are, they are useless without the knowledge of how to refine, combine, and deploy them. This is what intelligence refers to as "intangible technology." The CSIS memos claimed that "foreign students and scientists... at our academic institutions, research organizations, international conferences and high-technology companies will remain an efficient means of acquiring technical expertise in fields of dual-use applicability." CSIS went on to complain that it is powerless to intervene because of the lack of Canadian regulation regarding the transfer of expertise.

Guns and Ammunition

In general, guns and ammunition are much more strictly controlled in Canada than they are in the United States. Except for police, sport shooters, and a few permitted civilians, handguns are strictly illegal. All automatic weapons are prohibited, as are semi-automatic assault rifles and several other special-purpose long guns. Legislation has recently gone into effect that will require all gun owners to obtain a government licence; within two years, every individual gun will have to be registered with the government. Furthermore, there are all sorts of laws about the storage of guns and the procurement and storage of ammunition. Canada is rapidly becoming an NRA nightmare, and it is rapidly becoming more difficult to legally acquire firearms.

Waging War From Canada
Why Canada is the perfect base for organizing, supporting, and conducting international insurgency

One benefit of all this pending legislation, however, is that there is a sudden glut of cheap and available illegal firearms. Canadians are anxious to get rid of weapons which are illegal and weapons for which they can't be bothered to pay the registration fee. In the main, this includes hunting rifles and shotguns. The market is currently flooded with black-market exchange in these weapons, and likely will be for the next couple of years until the new laws fully come into effect.

For historical reasons, there also exist in Canada vast privately owned caches of outdated military weapons. Typically, these range from WWI-era Lee-Enfields (which use the modern .303 round) to WWII era semi-automatics, which will fire a modern NATO round. Recently, an attempt to ship 23,000 such rifles from Canada to a Reno gunsmith was intercepted in what Canadian and American authorities called "the biggest ever gun-smuggling ring to operate along the border." As the new gun laws come into effect, hoarders will be increasingly desperate to get rid of these now-illegal caches. While not the newest technology, they remain well-made and useful weapons. Cuban insurgents were armed with such weapons (smuggled from Canada) to win the 1959 revolution — if they were good enough for Comrade Castro surely they are good enough for current insurgents. Canadian army bases and legions (veteran's clubs) are the usual source of finding out who has these caches for sale. Most small towns also have a poorly guarded armoury with a respectable cache of such weapons used to train cadets and reservists in infantry drill.

The usual source for more modern hardware is, however, the United States. Most arms smuggling is from there to Canada rather than the other way around. If your organization requires automatic rifles, large calibre sniper rifles, or rocket-propelled grenades, the normal route is to acquire them in America and ship them north across the border. Alternatively, these toys may be purchased by those with good diplomatic skills from Mohawk territories along the St. Lawrence River. There are other sources for such weapons in Canada, but they must be regarded with extreme caution and suspicion.

Handguns

Special mention should be made of handguns in Canada, for they occupy a strange place in the Canadian psyche and law. Generally speaking, Canadians consider handguns to be a particularly evil and American thing, and they don't like them around. The fact that the Canadian murder rate is a small fraction of that in the United States is widely attributed to the fact that handguns are, with a few extraordinary exceptions, strictly illegal.

Contrary to Canadian media reports, handguns are not easy to obtain in Canada. Moreover, those which are obtained are often too hot to handle. Following are two examples of handgun sales in Canada. The first was a well-made and maintained .38 purchased from a biker. With a box of shells, it cost $300.00 Canadian (about $200.00 U.S.). Within a couple of weeks, however, it was learned that the biker from whom the gun was bought from had, previously, obtained a box of the weapons from a Toronto police officer. For all practical purposes, that made the weapon unusable. Who knows what records were on the weapon, whether the biker and the kop had a deal, or if the whole thing was just a sting. The gun was thrown into the Toronto harbour without ever being fired. Most usable handguns in circulation have, at one time or another, been through the hands of police. In other words, they are too hot to handle. There are handguns available from crack dealers on the street, but most of these are ancient junk or

Waging War From Canada
Why Canada is the perfect base for organizing, supporting,
and conducting international insurgency

124

drilled-out starter pistols which are as likely to harm the user as they are the user's enemy.

The second example of a handgun puchase was a "loaner" from a Mohawk insurgency group — a gun borrowed for a particular task. This was a .22 semi-automatic which had been very nicely homemade in someone's machine shop. It had the advantage of having no serial number, vendor trail, or police history. Still, the fact that the gun had been loaned to others and could not be disposed of after the job made it more trouble than it was worth. This may seem overly paranoid to American readers, but the Canadian state will spare no effort on forensic testing and the linking of every handgun shot. A favourite police press release whenever a handgun is confiscated is a listing of every crime it was used for. Usually, the person holding the weapon at the time of arrest is charged with all of them. Oddly, this same scrutiny does not apply to rifles and shotguns, even if they have been cut down to fit in a pocket.

Courts frown on handguns, and any crime committed with one will draw additional charges (and lengthier sentences) than the same crime committed with a rifle or a shotgun. Moreover, Canadians have a severe and inexplicable aversion to the things. Any positive propaganda an organization has established will be destroyed if one of its operatives is caught with a handgun. Canadian sympathizers who think it cool that someone has a cache of rifles, RPG's, or Kalishnakovs will turn informer at learning he has a Saturday night special. It makes no sense, but what are you gonna do? It's a Canadian thing. Given their limited accuracy, military value, and overblown risk, I would advise any organization to think long and hard about obtaining handguns in Canada. If someone has just got to have one for a particular job, he should be very careful of his source. The cleanest thing is to arrange for one of his fellow fighters to smuggle a piece in from America rather than try to obtain one in Canada, where it may already have a long and well-charted history. Better yet, he can cut down a rifle or a shotgun.

Chapter Seven
Canadian Identity

"False documents are as important to terrorists and their organizations as guns and bombs — they are the tools that help them ply their international trade of death and destruction." — Steven Emerson, Executive Director, Terrorism Newswire Inc.

"The escape route for the World Trade Center bombers lay through southern Ontario [Canada], where airline tickets and new identification were waiting for them." — John Thompson, Mackenzie Institute

There are times in every terrorist's life when he or she would just like to be somebody else for a while. Perhaps the kops or the spooks are getting too close, or maybe they need a crystal-clear record for crossing the border into America or for obtaining that new firearms acquisition certificate. Maybe they'd just rather not rent that van or buy that fertilizer in their own name, or possibly they've had stern words with a rival faction. It may be that they'd like to go on a trip back to the homeland and would rather travel as a Canadian. It may be

Waging War From Canada
Why Canada is the perfect base for organizing, supporting,
and conducting international insurgency

128

that they would like to sit on the board of directors of a Canadian charitable foundation but have an embarrassing criminal record. Or, perhaps they need some professional credentials so they can attend that conference where that diplomat from their homeland will be speaking. There are endless reasons why the working warrior might need one or more Canadian identities.

Overview of Canadian Identity

Canadians are sheep when it comes to identity. All of them carry at least two pieces of government identity, even though no law requires them to. Worse, Canadians routinely show their identification to whoever asks for it, regardless of the fact that no one has the right to see it. Canadians spend half their lives reaching into their wallets and purses to show each other their identification. If they lived in Nazi Germany, they would be running up to SS officers asking, "May I show you my papers, please?" Some think this obsession with identity comes from Canadians, as a whole, not having one.

While Canadian public agencies are more reluctant than their American counterparts to share information amongst themselves, they are much more assiduous in collecting and checking it. This is the crux of Canadian identification. While it is easy to forge the basic Canadian identification, those forgeries are of extremely limited value unless they match information held in government databases. To take one example, the *de facto* national identifier, the Social Insurance Number, is child's play to create. If one works under that number, however, or starts a bank account, or files an income tax return, they will almost certainly be exposed at the end of the next fiscal year. Canadian identity is not so much about document forgery as it is about matching records. In most cases it is far preferable to allow the government to print a "real" identification rather than creating one's own. As we shall see, this implies that it is also far safer to assume the identity of an existing person than it is to attempt to create a new identity.

Strategy

The cover an operative chooses will depend on who he is, his background, and his intentions. If he just plans to hit a target of opportunity, or get a job at the 7-11 until he can save enough money to buy that new barrel of fertilizer he has been dreaming about, then a quick and dirty ID should do the trick. If he intends to work long-term for his organization in a public role, greater care is needed. In either case, it is far preferable to assume the identity of a citizen rather than a landed immigrant, visitor, or refugee claimant, if only because it allows him to obtain travel documents and guarantees him re-entry into Canada should he be called away. For this reason, only spoofing citizenship will be dealt with in this chapter.

The first choice an operative must make is whether he wishes to be a born citizen or an immigrant who has been granted naturalized citizenship.

In general, it is best for him to assume the identity of a Canadian citizen from Ontario if his first language is English. This is simply because Ontario is by far the most populated province and has by far the greatest volume of records. Several people are certain to share any given name, and there is much less probability that the aunt of the person whose identification he is assuming also happens to be a file clerk at the provincial registry. Ontario also has the highest number of non-white citizens and those for whom English is a second language. In short, he is less likely to attract attention by being from Ontario, even if he doesn't live there now. If his first lan-

Waging War From Canada
Why Canada is the perfect base for organizing, supporting,
and conducting international insurgency

130

guage or his background is French (including Haitian and West-African) the same reasoning dictates that his identification should be from Quebec, which is the second most populous province and is also mainly Francophile. For these reasons, the following information will assume his new identification will be of a citizen born or naturalized in Quebec or Ontario, although what is said remains generally true of any province.

One note about application forms for the various documents discussed below: with the exception of passport applications, all of them can be obtained on the World Wide Web. Indeed, most Canadian government business can be conducted online. Rather than tediously list a bunch of URLs, however (which are likely to change before this goes to print) they may all be found on the main page of the issuing government. The operative can go to a search engine such as www.yahoo.ca and type in "Government of Canada," "Government of Ontario," or *"Gouvernement du Quebec"* to locate the official main page, then follow the ministry or departmental links or do a search from there. If he can fight a war, one can assume he can find a web page.

Finding a Mark

As mentioned above, it is far more preferable to assume the identity of a Canadian citizen than it is to create a fictional identity. The person whose identity the insurgent will assume will be referred to as the "mark." Time spent selecting and researching a good mark will pay off when the going gets rough. Before looking at some excellent sources for finding marks and obtaining data about them, let us examine the attributes of a perfect mark.

The perfect mark...

1. is a citizen of Canada, preferably by birth.

2. is still alive (see the section below about tombstoning). Ideally, they no longer live in Canada. If they do, they should now live in a different province of Canada than the fighter does.

3. has a low data profile. The terrorist's mark should live a simple, undocumented life. Unless fraud is his aim, his mark should live pay cheque to pay cheque. This will mean they likely have a small, private-sector data profile, which is based upon financial instruments and exchange. It will also mean they have likely never applied for a passport (most Canadians have not), since they do not have the money to travel overseas.

4. is demographically similar to the operative (age, sex, ethnicity).

5. is physically similar to him, (height, eye and hair colour).

6. is culturally and linguistically the same as him. At minimum, his mark and he share the same first language.

7. has a common name for someone of that cultural and linguistic background. It should not raise an alert if he and his mark are duplicate names in someone's database.

8. has never been charged with a crime. Anyone charged with a serious offence will have a fingerprint or even a DNA profile on file.

9. has a good credit rating or, better yet, no credit at all. The last thing the operative wants is collection agencies calling him for the sins of his mark.

Waging War From Canada
Why Canada is the perfect base for organizing, supporting,
and conducting international insurgency

132

Finding and Researching a Mark

There are reams of information about the art and science of selecting and researching a mark. I will not attempt to replicate those worthy labours here, except to mention a few sources uniquely suited to Canada.

Ex-pats

Because Canadians remain under the tyranny of that inbred clan of prostitutes known as the Royal Family, they have a close relationship with the United Kingdom. In practical terms, this means a lot of people born in Canada are raised in Britain, where they become naturalized citizens and never return. These are excellent marks for the simple reason that — except for birth registration — they have zero data profile in Canada. They are a blank slate for someone to draw upon with virtually no chance of conflict or exposure. To a lesser extent, this is also true of born Quebecois who are now citizens of France, or of Canadians who moved to the United States at a young age.

Here are some likely places to find Canadian ex-pats:

1. Foreign Who's Who directories, which often state place of birth.

2. Academia. Many scholars emigrated to foreign universities with young children. One can search university archives for faculty announcements of the approximate era.

3. Long-term diplomatic staff. Many dip-kids become naturalized citizens and remain in the countries to which their parents brought them.

Religious Communities

There are a few religious communities in Canada which live in self-contained communes and have for many generations. The largest of these, the Mennonites, are similar to the Amish. They might be Amish; who knows what planet they came from or why. No matter. The point is that these simple, devout Christians make really good marks.

Assuming the operative is a white English speaker, Mennonites satisfy most of the conditions listed above for the ideal mark. Those who live in their commune disavow modern technology, consumerism, and bureaucracy. As a result, they have a very low data profile. They do not drive cars and will not have a driver's licence. They will not likely have credit cards. They will almost certainly have no criminal record or collection agency problems. A lot of them share common names. They generally remain in the orbit of their communities except for an occasional trip to town to buy provisions and triple-X porn. Except for a few who do overseas aid work, they will almost certainly never have obtained a passport.

Community Health Centres

Community health centres are, as the name suggests, neighbourhood clinics that provide a limited range of medical services. Without exception, the databases of these centres are the ultimate resource for a Canadian-identity seeker. One can't praise them enough. Here are a few of the many reasons why:

- The health centres are tailored to a specific community. The clients of a health centre are the people who live in the

Waging War From Canada
Why Canada is the perfect base for organizing, supporting,
and conducting international insurgency

134

neighbourhood. If you need a Jamaican identification, you can get one from a health centre in a Jamaican neighbourhood. The same applies for Italian, Portuguese, Somalian, and just about every other cultural or racial group you care to name. There are even health centres (Oh God, stop drooling) that cater to Mennonite communities. The point is that the fighter can find a mark with the same background and demographic as himself.

- Health centres collect a lot of data. Besides having a complete demographic profile of the patient, including age, sex, language, income, history, and copious notes and diagnoses, the health centre record will often have everything you need to obtain the full identification kit. This includes place of birth, parents' names, health card number, SIN number, and hundreds of other facts and figures, which will allow someone to quickly and credibly assume identification. Records may be located — as with any database — by querying on one or more attributes. The health centres have hundreds to tens of thousands of records — the perfect mark is certain to be among them. More likely, there will be dozens of perfect marks.

- Health centres are administered by clinicians and volunteers. They can seldom afford to hire anyone who knows how to maintain a secure database, therefore so many practitioners, volunteers, and staff access the databases that security is non-existent when compared to government, university, or hospital databases.

"So, Mike," I hear someone saying, "where do I get me one of those community health centre databases?" This is not a book about hacking, but here are a few things to consider:

- These databases are usually developed on shrink-wrapped software applications (i.e., Microsoft database server, SQL server, Oracle) by third party vendors. Health centres generally contract these vendors for remote database support and maintenance, since they cannot afford to hire info-tech staff. This support is generally done through dial-in access. The health centre modem is almost always set to receive at any time, since this support is often done across time-zones. The dial-in number is usually a few digits higher or lower than the published fax-machine number. The communication application is always a shrink-wrap, usually PC Anywhere. The dial-in password is usually a variant on the name of the health centre. One can usually get in without knowing the password.

- Some maintenance and support cannot be done via modem, and the vendors routinely visit the health centres to have a look at the database or upgrade the application running it. The vendor companies have very high staff turnover. They seldom have company identification and are never asked for it if they do. The community health centre staff are warm, welcoming people — they will be all to happy to log someone on if he has "forgotten" his password. They might even lend him a zip disk if he needs to make a copy of anything.

- Once someone has the database, he will be disappointed to learn that it is encrypted. The key is almost always eight characters or less, and usually an English word. The key is not needed if he is running the database from the application it was designed for (although a user name and password for the application is). There are usually hundreds of application passwords created by non-technical

Waging War From Canada
Why Canada is the perfect base for organizing, supporting,
and conducting international insurgency

136

users. The default application username and password
(usually admin/admin or user/user) usually remains active.
Either the application passwords or the database key can
be cracked by a brute force application. Brute force applications and libraries can be downloaded off the web. The
key will be the same for all databases of all health centre's
running any version of that application.

Tombstoning (Not)

Various writers on identity fraud have suggested using the
vital statistics of a deceased person — usually a child — as the
basis of an identification. That may work in Kansas, but not in
Ontario. Just as each birth is registered with the Registrar
General, so is each death. Doctors or coroners must do this
upon pain of losing their licences or worse. Death certificates
and birth certificates are issued by the same provincial ministry under the same provincial act. The data is contained in the
same database and before a birth certificate is issued, the files
are automatically queried to ensure the person is not dead.
Someone can, if next-of-kin, executor, or estate trustee, obtain
the birth certificate of a dead person, but why would he want
to, except to obtain a Citizenship Certificate as previously described? A precursory check would reveal the situation. Besides, it's bad karma for a soldier to be carrying the identification of a corpse.

Canadian Citizenship

Being a citizen in Canada allows the following privileges:

1. One cannot be deported, unless it is proven one lied on one's citizen application.

2. One may vote in elections or run for public office.

3. One may obtain a Canadian passport.

4. One may re-enter Canada from abroad.

5. One can apply for certain public service jobs, even those which allow access to sensitive records.

6. One may travel to many allied countries (i.e., U.S.A.) without the need to obtain a visa or passport.

Except for a mandatory duty to file tax claims, there are few disadvantages to being a Canadian. There is no compulsory military service. Some countries (i.e., Japan) disallow dual citizenships and will revoke citizenship should a former national obtain Canadian citizenship, but Canada will not inform those countries if an immigrant becomes naturalized. It is permissible to be a dual citizen of both Canada and the United States, and tens of thousands of Canadians hold American citizenship even if they seldom or never go there. Recently, many Canadians have also been applying for Irish citizenship — it is remarkably easy to get for those with an Irish ancestry and allows the holder to work or conduct business throughout the European Economic Community. The advantages of this are obvious if someone happens to be a surviving member of the Red Brigade.

Waging War From Canada
Why Canada is the perfect base for organizing, supporting,
and conducting international insurgency

138

Born Citizen

Ironically, the easiest identity to assume is that of a Canadian citizen who was born here or born overseas to a Canadian parent. If someone is under 40 years of age, he may plausibly assume born citizenship regardless of his racial or cultural background — Canada has been truly multicultural for that period of time. It gets trickier, however, if his first language is not English or French. If he speaks with a foreign accent, it is possible that he was born a Canadian citizen and raised elsewhere, or that he was born overseas to a Canadian parent. It's a tradeoff: it may raise some official eyebrows, but it is far easier to obtain the documents in this situation than it is for those of a naturalized citizen. The core identification of the born Canadian citizen, upon which all other identification is built, is the birth certificate (or its equivalent) and the Social Insurance Number. Their core travel document is, of course, the passport.

Naturalized Citizen

A naturalized citizen is a landed immigrant who has been granted citizenship by waiting five years with no serious criminal charges and passing a test delivered by a citizenship judge. Anyone of any background and any age may plausibly be a landed immigrant, and if someone speaks with a heavy Swahili accent, this is probably the identity he should assume. A naturalized citizen enjoys the full privileges and protections of a born citizen. Their core identification is a citizenship certificate and a Social Insurance Number. Their core travel document is the passport.

Ontario Birth Certificate

Whenever a baby is born in Canada, the hospital, midwife, or doctor who delivered the baby registers that birth with the Registrar General of Ontario. At any time in his or her life, that person may obtain a birth certificate, which virtually all born Canadians carry in their wallet. The birth certificate is issued by the Government of Ontario or in whichever province the person was born.

There are two forms of birth certificates in Ontario: the long form — which contains detailed registry information, and the small laminated card — which most people have. This contains the name of the person, date of birth, birthplace, date of registration, date of issuance, Registrar General number, sex of registrant, and a registration number. It is printed in blue on Canadian Bank note paper, and is considered in and of itself to be proof of citizenship.

My birth certificate was last replaced in the 1980s and the laminate has already yellowed, making it hard to see the document underneath. There is no photograph or signature, and the document itself is printed in one colour only. Obviously, it would not be difficult to make a convincing forgery of such a document. Such a forgery would be useful for the purposes of obtaining some secondary identification or obtaining a mail drop-box, but not much else. The fact remains that the information on a fictional birth certificate would not match the information held in the Registrar General's database. It would not, in short, survive rudimentary scrutiny. It could not be used to obtain a Social Insurance Number or a passport. It would not withstand a routine police check through CPIC. It is, on the whole, useless.

Waging War From Canada
Why Canada is the perfect base for organizing, supporting,
and conducting international insurgency

140

The way to get a Canadian birth certificate is to get the province to print one. Below, it will be discussed how to find a mark whose identity can be assumed. The following information about the mark must be obtained:

1. Name

2. Date of birth

3. City, town, or village of birth

4. Sex

5. Father's name

6. Mother's maiden name

As long as this information closely matches that held by the registrar, one may mail away for the certificate or have it printed while one waits at an office of Consumer and Commercial relations. There is nothing alarming about obtaining replacement birth certificates for oneself — people lose them all the time. One may also obtain a birth certificate for a child of any age if one is a parent named in the registry.

Quebec Birth Certificate

The process in Quebec is exactly as described above, except that there is a parallel system administered by the Catholic Church. A baptismal certificate is given the same identification credibility as a government-issued birth certificate. This is not really a loophole, however, since the data is registered with the *Archiviste General* in the exact same manner as above. There is no advantage in obtaining a baptismal certificate instead of a secular birth certificate. If anything, there is a slight disadvantage in that the data must match against two sets of files: the secular ministry who issues birth certificates and the loftier ministry and their parish records. Also, carrying a baptismal certificate may be frowned upon by Allah and other comrades in the *Jihad*.

An Interesting Exception

Indian bands located in Ontario have their own civic administration, and may issue (through the Federal Department of Indian Affairs) an Indian Status Card which has the same functional value as a birth certificate. Interestingly, these are issued without checking for a corresponding registration made with the provincial Registrar General or *Archiviste General*. Nor, if CSIS were to perform such a check, would a lack of correspondence indicate identification fraud, since not all Indians — particularly those over thirty years of age — are registered births with the province. There is a weakness in the system here, and the Department of Indian Affairs has recently complained that they are powerless to fix it because the whole issue is too "political."

Citizenship Certificate

For those who cannot credibly claim to be a born Canadian but still wish to acquire the identification of a Canadian citizen, the document which must be obtained is a Citizenship Certificate. This is issued by the Government of Canada (Department of Citizenship and Immigration) and is carried by most naturalized citizens just as most born citizens carry their birth certificate.

Waging War From Canada
Why Canada is the perfect base for organizing, supporting,
and conducting international insurgency

142

It is much more difficult to obtain a Citizenship Certificate than it is a birth certificate. Far more supporting documentation is required, it is checked far more thoroughly — especially if someone immigrated from a country known to have insurgents operating in Canada — and the document itself is more sophisticated. The reason the Citizenship Certificate is more difficult to get is because it is administered by the Federal government, which tends to be more thorough in these matters than the provinces.

That being said, it can be done. It is done all the time. The requirements for documentation vary according to the place of birth, the year of birth, the sex and marital status, the citizenship of the applicant's parentage, and whether or not the applicant is a British subject. I will not go into the documentation requirements of each possible permutation, but there is a kit which may be downloaded from the Government of Canada (Department of Citizenship and Immigration) web site which does. There is, however, an easier route — although it leaves one to find a mark who suits it and do the extra homework required to make such a complicated application.

The first thing one should know about obtaining a Citizenship Certificate is that it is against the law to have more than one. More importantly, a duplicate request will raise an alert. Therefore, one must choose one's mark very carefully: he or she must be a naturalized citizen who has never applied for the document. Documents do get lost, of course, but to apply for a replacement one must provide one's original naturalization papers. This is going to be tricky.

Photographs

Unlike the birth certificate, an application for the Citizenship Certificate requires that a photograph be sent. This picture may be visually matched against the photograph on the original immigration or naturalization record of the mark. There will be years — or even decades — between the two photographs, but even that is not long enough to account for blue-eyed blonde-haired Svend Norsen suddenly looking Chinese.

The Path of Least Resistance

The easiest Citizenship Certificate requirement is for a person born outside Canada to a Canadian parent. Such a person would not, obviously, have a birth certificate or a birth registered with the province. Here is what would be required:

1. A birth certificate that lists the parents, issued by the government in the country in which one was born. It is required then to obtain a birth record from the country of the mark's birth. This is generally no more difficult than obtaining an Ontario birth certificate, although requirements vary. In general, poorer nations will issue such a document when and if it suits them, with little concern about security, while more developed bureaucracies will at least run the same sort of cursory check that Ontario does.

2. The Canadian birth certificate of the parent from whom one inherits Canadian citizenship. This may be obtained by the process above — either by masquerading as that per-

Waging War From Canada
Why Canada is the perfect base for organizing, supporting,
and conducting international insurgency

144

son if they are still alive, or by applying for the record as next-of-kin if they are dead.

3. A minimum of two pieces of personal secondary identification. The feds like to see a driver's licence and a health insurance card (both issued by the province) which we will discuss below. Other secondary provincial documents such as marriage certificates or legal name change certificates may also be included to boost credibility or — more likely — in lieu of a driver's licence.

The Application Form

It will be seen by anyone who downloads the application kit for obtaining a Citizenship Certificate that there are far more traps involved than just being born there. There are a lot of personal questions which could, in theory, be checked at issuance. More likely, they will be checked at some moment of crisis in the future and, if they don't stand up, they can bring someone's whole world crashing down around them. The key is the proper selection of the mark, and any time spent in research at the outset might save worlds of trouble down the road. This is particularly true if an operative intends to work and live in Canada in the long term or in a public capacity. An underground or silent operative may get by with the minimum, but if he is going to be a front-man for the cause — who will attract attention and enemies — he needs bulletproof identification. (More on selecting and researching a mark on page 130.)

The Social Insurance Number (SIN)

The *de facto* national identifier of any resident of Canada, (including citizens, landed immigrants, and refugee claimants) is the Social Insurance Number. Originally started for the purpose of administering unemployment insurance, its use has widened dramatically in scope. While only a few institutions can insist upon having your SIN, it is in fact freely asked for and freely given for all manner of private and public sector businesses. For some mysterious reason, this does not worry Canadians.

Along with a birth certificate or other proof of citizenship, one must have a Social Insurance Number or one will stand out. Even children and refugee claimants have them, and there is a whole range of normal activity, such as getting a job, starting a bank account, or filing income tax, that are impossible without it. For this reason it is also a primary identifier, along with name and date of birth, on the police CPIC database.

Oddly enough though, while a Social Insurance Number is necessary, one does not need the white plastic card (issued by the Government of Canada, Department of Human Resources Development) with the number embossed on it. Knowing the number itself is far more important than having the document which bears it. I personally lost my card as an adolescent and have never bothered to replace it. In the hundreds of times I have been asked by banks, government officials, police, and employers for this number, they have never actually asked to see the card. Thus, for some purposes, such as getting a short-term job or opening a short-term bank account, it is enough to create a seemingly valid number. This is described on the next page. For longer-term projects, however, an insurgent will

Waging War From Canada
Why Canada is the perfect base for organizing, supporting,
and conducting international insurgency

146

need to actually obtain a number with information that matches the federal government database. It is not difficult. The requirements for obtaining a real and valid SIN are minimal, so much so that the Auditor General recently carped that the government of Canada has issued millions more valid SIN cards than there are people in Canada.

Creating a SIN

For obtaining a short-term job or opening a bank account long enough to make a money transfer, one may simply make up a number which will survive a precursory arithmetical screening. Such a number will not survive matching Federal Government databases, and for this reason, it is for emergencies and very short-term usages. Indeed, giving such a number to an employer is the primary means by which the government identifies illegal immigrants working in Canada. A fake number should only be used for a matter of weeks or a couple of months at most. It will certainly show up at the end of a fiscal year and likely much sooner. Still, it can be useful. Certainly, it is better to have a few fake but initially convincing SIN numbers memorized (if a person has to look at his card, he is not Canadian) than to have none at all.

Structure

The SIN number is nine digits long. For refugee claimants and landed immigrants, the first digit will be "9." For Canadian citizens, the first digit will identify the region of the country in which the card was issued. For Ontario, this number is "4." The final digit of the SIN number is a check digit which arithmetically verifies that the number is valid.

Luhn's Formula

The arithmetical requirements of the SIN are that they satisfy Luhn's formula. Many computer systems employed by banks, employers, and government agencies likely to ask for one's SIN are coded so that they will not accept a number which does not fulfill this formula. The following is the process which checks the validity of a SIN:

1. A SIN number is entered. We will use the valid example of "550911895." Apologies in advance to whoever actually owns this number.

2. Disregard the final check digit, leaving "55091189."

3. Isolate every second digit, leaving "5," "9," "1," and "9."

4. Multiply each of these by two, leaving "10," "18," "2," and "18."

5. Cross-add this result, meaning that one totals all single digits $(1 + 0 + 1 + 8 + 2 + 1 + 8 = 21)$, leaving "21."

6. Add the digits left behind in Step 3 $(5 + 0 + 1 + 8 = 14)$, leaving "14."

7. Add the result of Steps 5 and 6. $(21 + 14 = 35)$, leaving "35."

8. Subtract the result of Step 7 from the next largest number ending in "0." $(40 - 35 = 5)$, leaving "5."

9. The result of Step 8 is the same as the SIN check digit ("5"). Therefore, the SIN number is valid.

Waging War From Canada
Why Canada is the perfect base for organizing, supporting,
and conducting international insurgency

148

Obtaining a Real SIN Number

A real SIN card may be obtained in person, at an unemployment centre office, or by mail. The government prefers the first, but an insurgent will likely prefer the last. If obtaining one's SIN by mail, an address should not be used which is obviously a drop-box. Only two documents are required: a birth certificate, passport, or some other proof of citizenship or residency, and a secondary identification. As mentioned above, SIN cards are issued to refugee claimants fresh off the airplane, so not a lot of scrutiny goes into them. I once got one with a birth certificate and a library card, but that was a few years ago and things are a little tighter now.

Passports

There is nothing like a Canadian passport to convince Customs agents abroad that you are a polite, harmless, docile little creature who wouldn't dream of taking hostages. Mossad murder-squads use Canadian passports — why shouldn't anyone else who needs one?

The operative — or his mark — must be a Canadian citizen to obtain a passport, but a passport is not in itself proof of citizenship. Rather, it is a travel document. Canada has good international relations with just about everybody, and a Canadian passport will allow an operative to obtain a travel visa for just about anywhere. Equally important, it will guarantee his re-entry into Canada even if Interpol is right behind him.

Forged Passports

Passports are well-made documents that include a laminated photograph and almost fifty internal security codes and devices. They are difficult to forge. Nevertheless, if an organization has the ability to create or — more likely — alter stolen passports, then passports are an exception to the "no forgery" rule above. In routine usage they are not measured against any database as the birth certificate and the SIN number are, and they are generally used as identification by foreign officials rather than other Canadians. Indeed, if travelling in North America, there is no need to obtain a passport, since neither the U.S., Cuba, Mexico, or most Caribbean countries require one from people entering from Canada.

If an organization doesn't have the ability to make a passport, others can make them for it. In a public report, CSIS claims that one of the fundraising activities of the Liberation Tigers of Tamil Eelam is the "manufacture and sale of false passports." One could find a nice Tamil printshop in Toronto and mention Second Lieutenant Malathi as a reference. Bikers are also reputed to be in the passport-making business, although in some people's minds, bikers and kops are a little too cozy and they wouldn't trust them. One can readily buy stolen passports for the purposes of alteration. Not to give the game away, but look for a cryptic ad in the alternative weekly newspapers of Toronto, Montreal, or Vancouver. Also, many down and out Canadians will obtain a passport and sell it. Make sure they can handle the inevitable questioning by police when they report it stolen. A comrade did this once and police interrogated him on the "theft" on two occasions for almost an hour.

Waging War From Canada
Why Canada is the perfect base for organizing, supporting,
and conducting international insurgency

150

Real Passports

Real passports may be obtained through the mail. To accelerate the process (and therefore cut down on the scrutiny which goes into issuing the document) an operative may contrive some sudden family emergency overseas. He can take this sad story to the constituency office of his federal member of Parliament, and he or she will be able to get him a passport very quickly. The application form for a passport — which he will need whether his MP is involved or not — may be obtained at any post office.

The documents required to obtain a passport are proof of citizenship (birth certificate or citizenship certificate as described above) and secondary identification. These must be real documents, but obtaining them is not difficult. More problematic is the requirement for the signature of a guarantor, that a person is who they say they are and bears a likeness to the photograph submitted with the application. The guarantor must be a Canadian citizen with no criminal record, they must be a member of a professional body, and they must vouch that they have known the applicant for two years. Not all guarantors are contacted to verify their signature on an application, but some are. This is particularly true, I'm afraid, for non-white applicants.

What to do? If an organization is well-established or large they will have members and sympathizers who will serve as guarantors. If they do not, they will have to find a Canadian who will. Bribery might convince them. If not, they might try threats.

One variant of obtaining a real passport is using someone else's. This may sound hard to believe, but there were some Chinese men who shared a passport between them for travel between Canada and Europe. They relied on the inherent racism of white, uneducated, and stupid customs officials to find that "they all look alike." It seems a bit risky, but I know for a fact that it has worked.

Seaman's Discharge

One excellent form of identification which is often overlooked by identity hunters is the Continuous Certificate of Discharge for Seamen. While not a common document (except among merchant mariners who work in international waters), it is remarkably easy to obtain and carries a high degree of credibility.

The Seamen's Discharge (yeah, yeah, I get it) is issued by the Government of Canada (Ministry of Transport) and can only be obtained in person at a Marine Customs House. It is a small booklet which looks much like a passport, but has none of the security controls. It is made while you wait, and the photograph is not laminated, but rather stuck on a page with a glue stick! It has no registration number and it is not entered into any database. Indeed, the only security control on the document is that one must sign one's name across the photograph and onto the page, and the Customs clerk does the same with her stamp. The document and the process for obtaining it are fabulously nineteenth century.

I once obtained a Seamen's Discharge for a friend, and I was amazed at how easy it was. A birth certificate and some secondary identification, along with a letter from the captain of the vessel to which one is signing on, confirming employment by him is all that is needed. A letter should also be mailed to the office in advance, notifying them of crew who will be obtaining Discharges (list a few people other than

Waging War From Canada
Why Canada is the perfect base for organizing, supporting,
and conducting international insurgency

152

oneself). These letters are from the captain of any vessel which will land in an international (including American) port. I created a letterhead for one of the many fake steamboats which take tourists to attractions on both sides of the St. Lawrence River, and got the captain's name from a company brochure. Although staff on these boats aren't required to have a Discharge, those who intend to pursue a marine career often do, and the Customs clerk didn't bat an eye. The whole thing took ten minutes. In fairness, I should point out that this was almost six years ago. To the best that I have been able to determine, however, the process is unchanged.

For a document that is so easy to obtain and alter, the Seamen's Discharge carries remarkable authority. In Canada, officials regard it as the equivalent of a passport, largely because it is a federal government document which bears a photograph, a signature, and an official stamp. Most federal documents (e.g., passports, Citizenship Certificates) do have a relatively high security threshold. The Discharge does not. Also, with its faux leather binding and bank-note pages, it just *seems* secure, and the fact that most provincial officials have never seen one makes it impressive by its novelty. Foreign officials often look at it as the equivalent of a passport, especially if one arrives by sea. In many countries, a Canadian Seamen's Discharge will get one waived through Customs.

Secondary Documents

The application for a SIN and a passport require secondary documents. Some of these, such as health cards and driver's licences, may be useful in their own right. A credible identity will have dozens of documents issued by government ministries, agencies, or businesses. Looking through this author's wallet, including credit cards, almost twenty pieces of special-purpose identification were found, ranging from library to health cards. That would be typical of most Canadians, and it is sadly typical that most Canadians carry these papers with them wherever they go. Following are brief descriptions of various secondary identification, their purpose, and things one must be aware of in seeking to obtain them.

Health Cards

Unlike the anarcho-capitalist evil empire to the south of us, Canada has a civilized health care system whereby anyone with a health card is entitled to free medical care. These cards are issued by the Provincial Government (e.g., Government of Ontario, Ministry of Health) and every Canadian, landed immigrant, or refugee claimant will have one. Besides their obvious utility in actually obtaining health care should one need it (God forbid), one's identity is not really credible without it.

Until a few years ago, obtaining a health card was as easy as walking into an office, showing one's birth certificate, and thanking the nice lady at the desk. It has since become a lot more complicated than that, largely because thousands of Americans from border towns were obtaining them and coming here for health care. Now, the Ontario cards bear a photograph and they require far more supporting documentation to obtain them. I will not go into the requirements, but they are available online from the Ministry of Health of the province in which an operative's mark lives. It seems onerous, but it is not. The application will only be checked against provincial databanks, and a proof of residence may be established with easily obtained private-sector identification and documentation.

Waging War From Canada
Why Canada is the perfect base for organizing, supporting,
and conducting international insurgency

154

Driver's Licence

Most Canadians own and drive cars, and to legally do so one must have a driver's licence. This is issued by the Provincial Government (e.g., Government of Ontario, Ministry of Transportation) or by private-sector contractors issuing the document on the government's behalf. Chances are the operative's mark will have a licence, so if he obtains one it will be a matter of replacing the two-part, photograph-bearing document rather than going through the tests to obtain one for the first time.

I advise against obtaining a driver's licence in the name of a mark for the following reasons:

1. The document contains both a photograph and a written description of the holder. The problems are obvious if one is obtaining a replacement document and does not match that description.

2. Driver's licences are the chief means of social control and data surveillance in Canada. Everything from child support payments to court fines and debts are linked to driver's licence renewal. Worse, the federal government grabs licence renewal and issuance data and compiles it in the CPIC databanks used by police. Because it is assumed that every adult resident of Canada, including refugee claimants, needs to drive, it has become the first tool for official sanction, surveillance, and investigation. It is the weak link of an identification profile, and it increases anyone's visibility a hundredfold.

3. The driver's licence number is the *de facto* Canadian business identification.

For the reasons above, I would advise anyone who lives in a city and is involved with a struggle against getting a driver's licence — even in their real name. The constant need for renewal means official databases are always being updated and one's history profiled. More importantly, Canadian police always pull over Canadian drivers on the pretext of looking for drunks, during which time they inspect identification and conduct searches of cars on the flimsiest of pretences. To search a pedestrian or an apartment requires much more work on their part (obtaining a warrant) and a written reason for their suspicions, which must withstand challenge in court. In short, Canadian drivers deal with kops all the time, and data about them is constantly being entered or queried in police and government databases. Canadians who do not have a licence (myself included) never deal with police unless actually apprehended in a crime. More importantly, the data profile is much smaller.

The vast majority of people who are busted in Canada for identification fraud get caught, in one way or another, by their driver's licence. Many people with genuine driver's licences get caught for their misdeeds, in one way or another, by their driver's licence.

Credit Cards

In many business transactions in Canada (e.g., renting a hotel room, starting a telephone account), the business will ask to see one's driver's licence. If a person does not have one, a credit card is almost always accepted as an alternative. Every terrorist should get a credit card.

Everyone is required to have a SIN number to open a bank account in Canada. If anyone has a bank account with any sort

Waging War From Canada
Why Canada is the perfect base for organizing, supporting, and conducting international insurgency

156

of a balance into which regular deposits are made, credit card applications will be foisted on the holder. There are reams of texts about credit card fraud and the like, but whether one intends to raise funds this way or not, a credit card is easy to obtain and a necessary part of a credible Canadian identification.

Throwaway Identification

An insurgent should fill out his identification package with easily obtained detritus that Canadians carry for special purposes. This includes such things as library cards, video-rental cards, photocopy cards, hospital or health clinic cards, staff or business cards, student cards, and the like. There is no reason to forge any of this. None of this stuff is essential in itself, but as a whole it provides credibility that he is who he says he is. He should especially seek anything with a photograph and a signature on it, as this impresses most business and government clerks regardless of who issued it or how easy it is to get. An excellent piece of photograph-bearing identification is a university student card. The terrorist may obtain one by registering for a course at any university. The university doesn't care who he is so long as he pays his tuition, yet this form of identification is considered as valid as a driver's licence for almost all purposes inside Canada, even after it is expired. If an insurgent takes a course in organic chemistry, he might learn something useful.

Chapter Eight
Legal Troubles

"Canada, for wanted people, is the safer place to live. ...there is much lower risk of detention and prosecution than in the United States or Europe." — Alfonso Caruana, "mafia boss," as quoted by Antonio Nicaso

"There is no easy way to investigate or prosecute a case involving different national laws, regulations, agencies, and political agendas." — American Department of Justice

If a fighter is seriously waging war from Canada, it is inevitable that he or some of his comrades are going to end up, at one time or another, with legal troubles. These could range from civil suits from a rival faction, criminal charges for not paying taxes on all that war-treasure he has been raising, or extradition proceedings initiated back home where they don't like what he did to that 747. While law is a huge subject and one about which I am by no means an expert, this book can offer some sound practical advice as well as an overview of Canadian law and its administration.

Waging War From Canada
Why Canada is the perfect base for organizing, supporting,
and conducting international insurgency

158

The Canadian Constitution

Until twenty years ago, Canada remained, in a legal sense, a colony of Great Britain. Any constitutional changes had to be approved by British Parliament and the ultimate court of legal appeals was the Privy Council in London. In the 1980s, Queen Elizabeth II — bless the poxed old drunken tart — signed the constitution over to Canada. An adjunct was the creation of the Canadian Charter of Rights and Freedoms.

The implications were huge. The ultimate legal authority was now the Supreme Court of Canada — composed of un-elected, irremovable, and non-partisan judges. They now had the power to strike out any law incompatible with the gener-ous terms of the Charter, and they began to do so with a fury. Moreover, that same court decided that anyone in Canada — even illegal immigrants — were subject to all the Charter protections and avenues of legal process available to Canadian citizens.

In practical terms, this has huge consequences for warriors using Canada as their base. Many criminal convictions can be appealed on constitutional grounds where, even if they have little hope in succeeding, they may serve as propaganda value or at least delay the inevitable. This arrangement also makes the quick removal of illegal aliens very rare; the Charter's rights of refugee claimants make the sort of deportations made under the United States expedited removal system virtually impossible.

There are numerous examples of revolutionary groups using the Supreme Court and the Charter of Rights to good effect. When the Canadian Progressive Conservative government tried to finish off the cold war by changing the Elections Act so that its old archrival the Communist Party of Canada would lose all its assets, the comrades appealed to the Supreme Court and the law was struck down. When Indian activists were accused of illegal fishing, they used the Supreme Court to reinstate treaties signed with the British before there was a Canada. Even if an insurgent's enemy is the Canadian state itself, the new Charter of Rights and Freedoms is a friend. It can be used against the bastards.

Canadian Criminal Law

Canadian criminal law is expressed in the Criminal Code of Canada, and applies equally to all parts of Canada. Lesser offences (the American equivalent of misdemeanors) are expressed in provincial statutes. Regardless of which law is broken, the initial trial will be in a provincial court.

It will be noted by anyone reading the criminal code that almost everything worth doing is against the law in Canada. There are even ancient laws such as the one against "intimidating the legislature." Moreover, even the most boring crimes usually carry (on paper) a ridiculously long maximum sentence. It shouldn't worry a warrior. Canadian judges are notoriously generous, and the maximum sentence — or anything near it — is very seldom imposed.

Canadian Civil Law

For legal disputes not involving the state, the relevant law depends on where someone lives. Quebec (French-speaking Canada) bases their civil law on the Napoleonic Code, whereas the rest of Canada bases theirs on British tort law. All civil courts also hear precedents set in civil courts in the

Waging War From Canada
Why Canada is the perfect base for organizing, supporting,
and conducting international insurgency

160

United States and throughout the commonwealth ("common law").

Because civil courts have a lower standard of proof than criminal courts, the provincial government is attempting to use the court to hurt criminal and insurgent organizations by suing them rather than criminally convicting them. This is a new idea to Canada and is unlikely to survive a Charter challenge. On the flipside, insurgents have made good use of civil courts to silence their critics or harm their enemies or rival factions. In one such example, FACT, an organization which the Department of Justice has listed as a terrorist front organization, is suing one of Canada's national newspapers for making the same claim. In their statement, FACT uses the language of the Charter of Rights, namely that the newspaper stories are "a denial of Tamil-Canadians' right to associate, assemble, and express themselves." It is unlikely that the suit will succeed, but it is of inestimable propaganda value. More importantly, the newspaper in question has stopped the damaging counter-propaganda against FACT.

Arrest

An insurgent's first introduction to the Canadian Criminal Code is likely to be an arrest made by municipal, provincial, or federal kops. Depending on the circumstances and the seriousness of that crime, an arrest could be made with a gentle touch on the shoulder or a full-scale para-military takedown. Regardless, the arresting officer is obliged to tell him upon arrest what crime he is charged with committing. If he does not do this, the fighter should make a mental note of it — he may be able to use it against him later.

Assuming that he intends to submit to the arrest, the only information he is obliged to give the police is his name and address. He should not, under any circumstances, give more information than this. I cannot stress this enough. Anything he says in his own favour will be ignored; anything that can be used against him or his organization will be used with a fury. The kops may beat him, interrogate him, and threaten him and his family. Nevertheless, he should say nothing except "I want a lawyer." The more they cajole him to talk, the more likely it is that their case against him is weak.

This bears repeating a thousand times: he should say nothing. Most criminal convictions in Canada are made on evidence supplied, often unwittingly, by the accused. When the RCMP first arrested — fifteen years ago — Talwinder Singh Parmer, the Sikh terrorist accused of bombing Air India flight 182, they held and interrogated him for days. Through it all he sat, cross-legged and silent, staring at the floor. He didn't say a word, and in spite of the evidence against him (i.e., CSIS had observed him testing bombs made of the same materials as the one used on the airplane), he was released. An arrested fighter should say nothing except "I want a lawyer." If he doesn't know a lawyer or can't afford one, he should ask for legal aid or duty council.

Charges

Charges in criminal matters are launched by the Crown in the person of Crown Prosecutors. They must be convinced by the police that there is a chance of conviction, and if the accused has said nothing at all to the police, that job will be much harder. Even if he was caught red-handed, the police and the Crown will be required to expend vastly more re-

Waging War From Canada
Why Canada is the perfect base for organizing, supporting,
and conducting international insurgency

162

sources on convicting him if they have no cooperation. Crown resources are tight, and it is possible to wear the Crown down this way — by making them spend a lot to obtain evidence and by making every possible motion and appeal. Indeed, some have got off criminal charges by extending the proceedings so long that the case has been thrown out on Charter grounds.

It is a long, slow grind to go through the court system, especially if the fighter is held in custody throughout his trial. The courtroom is an extension of the battlefield — he should use it to make propaganda in his testimony, never cooperate with his Canadian enemies (i.e., the police and the Crown) and always delay the proceedings as much as possible by contesting every procedure. The more money, trouble, and embarrassment he costs the system, the less likely the police and Crown prosecutors are to go after comrades in his organization. The model here should be Mohawk insurgents, and it is well worth the time to attend a few of their trials to see how experts use charges against them to further their cause. They do this by making endless costly (to the Crown) motions and by defending themselves on grounds that the court has no jurisdiction over them. Every motion and appeal is accompanied by press releases and demonstrations. Then, if convicted, they appeal the matter to the United Nations Human Rights Committee, further embarrassing the state which charged them. The end result is that the Crown is nervous about charging politically motivated Mohawks, and often tries to divert such cases to "mediation" rather than criminal proceedings.

Prison

If a fighter is convicted of a crime and sentenced to do time, he will be sent to one of two prison systems. For sentences of under two years, he will be sent to a provincial jail. If he can argue heavy familial responsibilities, he may be allowed to serve this sentence on weekends only. For longer sentences, he will be sent to a minimum, medium, or maximum security federal prison. Provincial and federal prisons are vastly different.

His time in a provincial prison will likely be spent in dormitories of up to forty bunks. The vast majority of his fellow inmates are just normal folk who got caught drunk-driving or for some other petty crime. They are generally not hardened criminals. There are not many recreational, educational, or work opportunities. Mostly people lay in bed, read books, watch television, play cards, smoke pot oil, and wait for their time to pass. He is well-fed, even getting snacks between meals. The guards will have as little to do with him as possible and will turn a blind eye to most things. After all, they have their own card games to play and their own oilers to smoke.

Most violence in provincial jails comes from mentally unstable people or over drugs. There is a lot of pressure to get drugs smuggled in by visitors or, alternatively, to bring in drugs should one be serving on weekends. The way to beat this is to have nothing to do with drugs from day one. No matter what one's past, never take a hit from anyone, pretend never to have done so, and pretend no knowledge of anyone who has. By taking this expediency, a prisoner will be largely protected against drug-related trouble. And, more likely to preserve his revolutionary credibility and discipline. Regardless, provincial prisons are not violent places when compared, for example, to U.S. state prisons. Troublemakers who do not enjoy the protection of organized inmate groups are quickly transferred to more secure federal jails.

If a fighter is sentenced to more than two years, his time will be spent in a federal institution. In some respects, these are

Waging War From Canada
Why Canada is the perfect base for organizing, supporting,
and conducting international insurgency

164

better places to live than provincial cans. He will live in a cell rather than a dorm, there are many recreational activities, and there are opportunities to work or go to school. On the flipside, the food is worse and he will be sharing his hotel with a different sort of people than he met in the provincial jail. What violence there is will be far more serious than the punch-ups he may see in provincial jail, and there are bound to be people who hate him. The guards will also take a more active interest in making his life difficult than in a provincial jail.

The racial divide in Canadian federal prisons is not so much black/white as it is Indian/white. Respect is the key. Cultur-ally, Canadian Indians tend to be quiet and seemingly with-drawn. Don't interpret that as weakness, submission, or sim-ple-mindedness, or one will soon be convinced otherwise. Rape is much less common in Canadian prisons than Ameri-can ones, though, of course, it happens. Usually, people will come to one's defence if one shows a willingness to fight back. If a person can cultivate a few friendships, stay out of drug wars, and never rat on anyone no matter how much they deserve it, it should be all right. There are definite rewards for working hard and being a "good" prisoner; early releases are decided by a civilian parole board whose main evidence is one's prison record.

Throughout it all, the fighter should remember that in serving his sentence he is still doing his duty to the cause. So long as he doesn't rat on his comrades or make a dishonourable deal with the Crown Prosecutor, the fact that he has been taken prisoner makes him no less of a soldier. Every great revolutionary has done his or her time in prison. Leon Trotsky was in a Canadian prison before returning to Russia to form the Red Guard into a fighting army. The insurgent should be like him, quietly recruiting allies without being obnoxious to those who don't care for his cause, maintain discipline, keep in shape, and plan the future of his struggle. As with prisons everywhere, one should try to get a job in the kitchen — one will eat better and other prisoners will be grateful for any fermentable scraps one can salvage. The fighter will have communications with the outside world (one of Canada's leading literary columnists writes from jail where he is serving 18 years for bank robbery), and confidential communications with his lawyer. He can continue to advance his cause in any way that he is able. At the same time, unless his enemy is the apparatus of the Canadian state, being a good prisoner will secure an earlier release and such perks as day-passes and job-postings on the outside. By law, he will be released on parole after serving two-thirds of his sentence unless there is overwhelming evidence that he is hell-bent on re-offending.

Removal or Deportation Orders

If an insurgent came to Canada on a visa and overstayed his visit, or if he came to Canada as a refugee claimant and that claim was denied, there may come a time when the Department of Immigration may issue a warrant for his removal or deportation. He needn't be sad. As Texas Congressman Lamar Smith said about Canada, "Even when a refugee claim is denied and the alien ordered deported, the deportation order is almost never carried out." People are deported, of course, but seldom the ones who are determined to stay.

If a person has reason to believe there is an immigration warrant against them, they shouldn't panic. They are in good company. There are tens of thousands of people in Canada living quite happily with deportation orders against them. The police force responsible for finding them (known informally

Waging War From Canada
Why Canada is the perfect base for organizing, supporting,
and conducting international insurgency

166

as the "Trackers") was disbanded in 1993. Other police forces haven't picked up the task. Ahmed Ressam, the Al-Quaeda terrorist caught smuggling millennial RDX into the U.S., had a deportation warrant against him when he was arrested by Montreal police. They did not act upon it. His partner, Abdelmajid Dahoumane, managed to live for a year travelling throughout Canada and the United States in spite of the fact that he was Canada's most wanted man. Eventually, he showed up back home in Algeria.

Here are the statistics on deportation: in 1998, there were 6,119 warrants for removal issued by Immigration. Six hundred and forty of those warrants were carried out. Two hundred and forty were cancelled. That leaves 5,272 of the warrants where there was, in government terms "no action." The odds are good, about ten to one, against a deportation order actually leading to an operative's removal, even if he subsequently is arrested by police over a Criminal Code matter. He can change his identity if he really fears his deportation order, but it is probably not necessary.

If his deportation order is acted upon, don't give up. Get the documentation required to board a plane, destroy it en route, and start all over again under a different name. There are hundreds of people in Canada who have had the misfortune to be deported over and over again. He can look at it as a holiday before getting back to Canada and back on the job. Another option is to plead for Ministerial compassion to lift the deportation order. This is often effective in cases where he can plausibly argue that he will be executed upon arrival in the old country, and it doesn't matter if the execution will be carried out by state or "terrorist" organizations. Canada abhors the death penalty and will not generally deport people to countries where they face it. If it is appropriate to his case, the terrorist can use that weakness to his advantage.

Extradition from Canada

Extradition proceedings — where a country which has an extradition agreement with Canada wishes to have someone returned home for a crime he committed there — are different than deportation orders. They will certainly be acted upon. His only hope of evading them is:

1. Staying on the lam. They can't extradite him they ain't got him.

2. Successfully arguing the proceeding (e.g., on the grounds that there is not enough evidence to extradite).

3. Compassionate grounds. Canada routinely refuses to extradite people to countries — including the United States — where they may face the death penalty. This is a useful piece of information to know should he be accused of killing someone in America. If he gets across the border, he may still do time, but there is no chair.

Extradition to Canada

Just as other countries ask for their terrorists and criminals back, Canada also initiates proceedings in other countries against persons alleged to have been bad in Canada. As in all extradition proceedings, diplomatic convention has it that a person can only be tried for the crimes for which he was extradited. In exceptional cases, this can be an odd advantage. To take a recent example, the Sikh warrior Inderjit Singh Reyat was extradited from England to Canada for his role in the Narita airport bombing. When Canadian police later attempted to charge him in the explosion of Air India flight

Waging War From Canada
Why Canada is the perfect base for organizing, supporting,
and conducting international insurgency

168

182, they found they could not because he had not been extradited for that crime. Oops!

The closest country to Canada that has no mutual extradition agreement is Panama. If shit really hits the fan, a fighter can make his way there and say "hi" to all the ex-Canadians he will find.

Conclusions and Comments

The national animal of Canada is the beaver, a large rat that lives in the water. The main characteristic of beavers is that they chew down trees and build dams with them. They will dam a small stream and turn the surrounding land into a lake. Farmers dynamite or bulldoze the dams, but the beavers that survive just start rebuilding the next day. They never surrender, even against overwhelming odds.

When I was a boy, I shot a beaver through the chest with a thick, barbed, fibreglass fishing arrow. The beaver looked up at me, made an angry gurgling sound, and started chewing on the arrow. He died, but not until he had broken my only arrow in half. I learned a lot from that beaver. I learned the importance of using your strengths to deprive the enemy of his, and I learned the importance of making him pay dearly for his every success. I learned that is was possible to lose a struggle without allowing your enemy to win it. I learned that, as long as there are those who will fight with unyielding single-minded determination, a lost battle will never be the same as a lost cause.

Waging War From Canada
Why Canada is the perfect base for organizing, supporting,
and conducting international insurgency

170

Who knows how an insurgent's struggle in Canada will end? It may end in shackles at the gates of the Kingston Penitentiary. It may end when he boards a plane to be deported back to the country where they will put him in the hands of a torture squad. It may end when he releases the clutch of his truck for that last drive to the consulate. It may end with the sudden blow of a sniper's bullet. Or, it may end with sentimental obituaries for the respected citizen who died in bed after working all his life for some "charitable" cause. However it ends, the warrior should make peace with his god if he has a god. And think of the beaver.

The struggle continues. Thank you for visiting Canada.

Canadian Glossary

BC: British Columbia. Province bordering Pacific Ocean. Capital is Vancouver, a dreary collection of crack-heads, Vietnam draft-dodgers, and deadbeat dads.

Beaver: National animal of Canada.

Bloc Quebecois: Political party dedicated to Quebec nationalism and independence.

Cabinet: Elected heads of government departments.

Canadian Alliance Party: Opposition political party in Canada. Pro-life, free-market capitalist, born-again Christian. Roughly equivalent to American Republican Party, but even more obnoxious.

CAW: Canadian Auto Workers. Richest and most powerful Canadian Union. Socially friendly and hungry for propaganda with a "human rights" angle.

CLC: Canadian Labour Congress. Umbrella organization of Canadian Unions. Excellent ally.

Waging War From Canada
Why Canada is the perfect base for organizing, supporting,
and conducting international insurgency

172

CPC: Communist Party of Canada. We will bury you.

CPIC: Canadian Police Information Centre. Maintains a police database available to every kop on the street. Now available to Intelligence and Immigration officials. Not hard to get access to, but of limited utility and accuracy.

CSIS: Canadian Security Intelligence Service. Civilian body responsible for spooking terrorists. Famous for their incompetence, but they rely heavily on American, English, and Israeli counterparts.

DND: Department of National Defence. Oversees army, navy, and air force.

FACT: LTTE front organization. Tony the Tamil Tiger says, "they're grrrreat!"

FLQ: Quebec Liberation Front. Back in its heyday, it was one of Canada's few exclusively domestic terrorist organizations. Bombed a lot of mailboxes and wasted a couple of pols before taking refuge in Cuba. Thanks, Fidel!

HRM: Her Royal Majesty Queen Elizabeth II. Constitutional Head of Canadian State.

INS: Yankee immigration kops.

IRB: Immigration and Refugee Board of Canada. Triumvirate responsible for deciding the validity of refugee claims. Mostly party hacks, drinking buddies, mistresses and boy-toys of cabinet ministers.

Jean Chretien: Prime Minister of Canada and leader of the Liberal Party of Canada.

KKK: see *SQ*.

Liberal Party: Political party which has maintained power in Canada for most of the 20th Century. Position is campaign left and rule right. Roughly equivalent to American Democratic Party.

LTTE: Liberation Tigers of Tamil Eelam. By far the most successful insurgency movement now active in Canada. Has had the Minister of Finance attend fundraisers and has had large school boards commemorate fallen comrades. Learn from them.

Mackenzie Institute: Canadian anti-terrorist think-tank.

Minister: An elected member of parliament responsible for a department of government; member of Cabinet.

Mohawks: Warrior/trader nation which lives along the St. Lawrence River and Lake Ontario. Canada's unofficial supplier of arms.

NDP: New Democratic Party. Nominally socialist political party. Equivalent to British Labour Party, except that they have no chance of ever winning a federal election.

Ontario: Most populated province in Canada. Begins at upstate New York, ends god knows where.

OPP: Ontario Provincial Police.

PKK: Kurdistan Worker's Party. You go, comrades!

PMO: Prime Minister's Office. This is the *politburo* of Canada and the centre of all political power.

Poutine: Explosive manufactured by the FLQ out of fats and other organic solids. Hard to detonate, but quite possibly the only edible explosive.

Waging War From Canada
Why Canada is the perfect base for organizing, supporting,
and conducting international insurgency

174

Prime Minister: *De Facto* Head of State. Roughly equivalent to German *Führer*.

Privy Council: The body made of elite politicians and bureaucrats. Ultimately responsible for all police, intelligence, and counter-terrorism. Better to influence them than fight them, unless your enemy is the Canadian state itself.

PROMIS: Secure RCMP/Intelligence database. Has been hacked by Mossad and the CIA.

Province: Semi-autonomous political division of Canada. Roughly equivalent to an American state. There are ten such divisions in Canada, and three Northern wanna-bes (Yukon, Northwest Territories, and Nunavut).

Provos: Provisional Irish Republican Army. Insurgent movement which once showed some promise before their unconditional surrender to HRM.

Quebec: French-speaking province of Canada.

RCMP: The Royal Canadian Mounted Police. The Mounties. Federal police force. Their duties range from issuing traffic tickets to spooking. More open to bribery/infiltration than provincial and municipal police. Also more susceptible to pressure via their political masters in the Privy Council.

RDX: Boom! Better than ice cream.

Ricin: A poisonous protein which occurs naturally in castor beans.

RPG: Rocket propelled grenade. Hard to buy in Canada except from Mohawks.

SIN: Social Insurance Number. This is the *de facto* national identifier, necessary for finding legal employment.

SQ: *Surete de Quebec*; Quebec Provincial Police. Beware of these fuckers, especially if you are not white. Incompetent, but brutal.

Toronto: The largest city and cultural centre of Canada. The only Canadian city of any importance.

U.S.: The Great Satan. Soft underbelly is called Canada.

YOU WILL ALSO WANT TO READ:

- ❑ **61114 REBORN IN CANADA, Personal Privacy Through a New Identity, 3rd Edition,** *by Trent Sands.* Canada offers many opportunities for the new identity seeker. The Canadian lifestyle is very similar to that of the United States, and Canada would be the easiest foreign country for an American to adopt. This is a complete guide to building a new identity in Canada from the ground up. This new edition covers changes in the licensing system, how to prove residency, how to set up "employment," and the "two-wallet system," an essential for anyone traveling back and forth between the U.S. and Canada, and much, much more. *1999, 5½ x 8½, 120 pp, illustrated, soft cover.* $15.00.

- ❑ **61172 REBORN OVERSEAS, Identity Building in Europe, Australia and New Zealand, 2nd Edition,** *by Trent Sands.* The walls between nations are crumbling, and that opens rare opportunities for those who need a new identity. The formation of the European Common Market has created a paper-tripping paradise. With an identity in any one nation, you can live, work, and travel in all twelve. This book shows you how to get all the documents necessary to build a complete paper identity without leaving the United States. You'll also learn how to fake education, employment, and credit references. *2000, 5½ x 8½, 108 pp, soft cover.* $16.00.

- ❑ **61168 THE ID FORGER: Birth Certificates & Other Documents Explained,** *by John Q. Newman. The ID Forger* covers in step-by-step detail all of the classic and modern high-tech methods of forging the commonly used identification documents. Chapters include: The use of homemade documents; Old-fashioned forgery; Computer forgery; Birth certificate basics; and other miscellaneous document forgery. *1999, 5½ x 8½, 107 pp, soft cover.* $15.00.

- ❑ **61163 IDENTITY THEFT: The Cybercrime of the Millennium,** *by John Q. Newman.* Your most valuable possession is what makes you *you* — your identity. What would happen if someone stole it? Each year, more than 500,000 Americans fall victim to identity theft, and that number is rising. In this comprehensive book, you will learn: how thieves use computer networks and other information sources to adopt, use, and subsequently ravage the identities of unsuspecting victims; what you can do to protect yourself from identity theft, and how to fight back effectively if you are one of the unlucky victims. *1999, 5½ x 8½, 100 pp, soft cover.* $12.00.

❑ **32060 DAVID'S TOOL KIT: A Citizen's Guide to Taking Out Big Brother's Heavy Weapons,** *by Ragnar Benson.* What do you do when faced with the overwhelming firepower of ruthless authority? *Fight back,* that's what! Ragnar Benson provides citizen defenders with the information they need to mount a successful campaign against overwhelming odds... *and win!* Brief histories of armed resistance and tank warfare are included. This may be the most essential self-defense book ever written! *1996, 5½ x 8½, 224 pp, illustrated, soft cover.* $16.95.

❑ **61139 METHODS OF DISGUISE, Revised and Expanded, Second Edition,** *by John Sample.* Here is an incredible, completely illustrated book on how to disguise yourself! Covers everything from "quick-change" methods to long-term, permanent disguises. Includes: how to assemble a pocket disguise kit you can carry with you and use at any time; ways to change your face, body shape, voice, mannerisms, even fingerprints; mail-order sources for make-up, wigs, elevator shoes, fake eyeglasses, and much more. This is the most comprehensive guide to disguise ever compiled! *1993, 5½ x 8½, 264 pp, illustrated, soft cover.* $17.95.

Please send me the books I have marked below:
❑ **61114, Reborn in Canada, $15.00**
❑ **61172, Reborn Overseas, $16.00**
❑ **61168, The ID Forger, $15.00**
❑ **61163, Identity Theft, $12.00**
❑ **32060, David's Tool Kit, $16.95**
❑ **61139, Methods of Disguise, $17.95**
❑ **88888, 2001 Loompanics Unlimited Main Catalog, $5.00 (***Free*** if you order any of the above titles)**

WWC

**LOOMPANICS UNLIMITED
PO BOX 1197
PORT TOWNSEND, WA 98368**

Please send me the books I have checked above. I am enclosing $ _____ which includes $5.95 for shipping and handling of orders up to $25.00. Add $1.00 for each additional $25.00 ordered. *Washington residents please include 8.2% for sales tax.*

NAME _____

ADDRESS_____

CITY/STATE/ZIP_____

We accept Visa, Discover, and MasterCard. To place a credit card order *only,* call 1-800-380-2230, 24 hours a day, 7 days a week.
Check out our Web site: www.loompanics.com